To Russell
from Polly

W9-CXZ-509

# *Letters Home and Further Indiscretions*

## BY FRANCIS COLBURN

THE NEW ENGLAND PRESS
SHELBURNE, VERMONT

The New England Press
P.O. Box 525
Shelburne, Vermont 05482

ISBN (cloth) 0-933050-00-3
ISBN (paper) 0-933050-01-1

Acknowledgments

"Sows' Ears and Purses" first appeared in *Centaur,* Vol. II, No. 3, Spring - Summer, 1960.

"Art and Change" first appeared in *The College Miscellany,* edited by Samuel N. Bogorad and Jack Trevithick (Rinehart & Company, Inc., New York, 1952).

Printed by Northlight Studio Press, Barre, Vermont
Designed by Cyndy Brady

PRINTED IN THE UNITED STATES OF AMERICA

# *Introduction*

I don't know who conned Francis into doing this book, but whoever it was has my abiding gratitude — and that of my children and grandchildren although they don't know it yet.

When a real estate agent writes about a house of singular nature, the copy usually ends up with the words "must be seen to be appreciated." Applied to Francis the line might go, must be seen and heard and read to be appreciated. Not that he's for sale. He is not and never has been. But his paintings can be acquired, his recordings purchased, and now his book can be bought. This means that a lot of people will be able to see and hear and read him for a long time to come. And they will remember, as Henry told his troops on Crispin's day, with advantages.

What advantages? Well, this book contains a man: husband, father, painter, musician, teacher, essayist, and humorist. A reader will be entertained, illuminated, and inspirited. What more can be asked of a book? Or a man?

Francis must have agreed to the publication of some of his letters to good, close friends with the same eagerness he would have displayed if asked to play his viola naked on Craftsbury Common in February. But the letters are warm and revealing and, in places, downright funny. The book would not have been complete without them. The prose pieces that follow the letters form a commentary on art and education that is full of sense and nonsense, passion and compassion — products of a mind as straight and uncompromising as a plumb line.

I would have bet money that his convulsively funny recording of the "Graduation Address" could not survive being written down. But in this book it not only survives, it triumphs.

"Confession of Faith," the concluding essay in the book, is a clear statement of what Francis Colburn believes to be the best answer to the challenge of living on this particular planet. The reader will not be surprised to learn that he insists that we take the hard road into our various imaginative, creative selves, rather than the easy way out.

Finally, it is somehow reassuring to know that a society which seldom recognizes its more important contributors has taken note of this one.

Keith Jennison
Castleton, Vermont

## Preface

As this book is launched, my rural emotions are mixed. I feel very much as I did when the University of Vermont requested a retrospective exhibition of my paintings some years ago. My soul was bared and I was forced to see where I had been and where I was to go.

The letters in this collection I wrote to my dear friends Frederick and Marjorie Smith, Robert and Ruth Kroepsch, Samuel and Ruth Bogorad and Robert and A. A. Babcock. Thanks go to Marjorie Smith who thoughtfully collected these letters and returned them to me. Thanks, too, to my wife who prepared the manuscript for publication.

Francis Colburn
July 5, 1978

*For Gladys*

# Contents

# *I. Letters Home*

Behold! After weeks of navigating, we are in California — safe in the arms of Jesus, David and Lorrie. Minor saints tended us on our way — Happy Dustan in Cleveland, the Dan Curleys in Urbana and the more than saintly Kroepsches in Boulder. Now here we see the Clement Hurds (remember?) and particularly Anthony Ostroff and lovely wife. He's a poet and on the University of California faculty. Yaddo alumnus. Gladys is, indeed, out at the moment with Posey Hurd calling on Sarah Bard Field, relict of Charles Erskine Scott Wood. She (Field) must be about a hundred seventy-five years old!

I have had the grand tour of the University of California Art Department and will now go back to visit classes in some depth. All the kids here are art majors and good — but I'm still proud of mine after all I've seen over this alarmingly BIG country.

After Urbana I had the opportunity to genuflect before Lincoln's home in Springfield. I stood on the very boards he did. (I hope.) Had a considerable discussion with Bob Kroepsch about the relative virtues (thrills?) of the real thing versus the authentic replica. Is it more breathtaking to sit on the *very* milking stool Walter Wheeler used, or on an authentic replica? Me, I'm glad Mark Twain's house in Hannibal is the original house — not a bunch of ersatz like Ticonderoga or Williamsburg. I suppose someday some authority will inform me that the boards Lincoln and I have trod together are phonies. Oh, well.

Kansas seemed flat. After leaving the Kroepsches we

went over the Rockies on a minor pimple called the Berthoud Pass. Ruthie Kroepsch assured us it was a breeze — and how right she was! We left Boulder in sunny, 70° degree weather and drove up, over and down Berthoud Pass in a blinding snow storm, a considerable gale, and on very slippery stuff. All over the road, that is. I assume I was on a road part of the time. Breeze, indeed! I was never so scared in my life. Mama, too. So, as I say, Kansas seemed *flat*. Anybody want to make something of that? It's a virtue, kids, a real *virtue*. To be sure, there are degrees of flatness and straightness — what I mean, I don't want to go overboard about this thing. Take the Great Salt Desert. Don't just stand there, *take* it. Over that I kept having the feeling that I'd been where I was before — like ten or fifteen minutes before. I was usually right, too.

Still, it *is* flat and doesn't make you want to urinate (or worse) all the time, as does Berthoud Pass. Apparently we both have a tendency to get giddy at any height greater than that of Craftsbury Common, Vermont.

In Utah I saw the first Indians I'd ever seen who weren't wheeled into the cigar store at night. It's hard to believe that my Great Uncle Ogden Read was one of their better known adversaries in the 1870's. They seem so nice.

And in Nevada I got so many silver dollars in change that I began to walk with a noticeable list to port until Gladys suggested I divide the cartwheels evenly between right and left pants pockets. I did. It worked. (Bright as a silver dollar, that one!) One of those dollars I shall keep for my Mem Book.

We went through Reno fairly fast, since we seem to be getting along together pretty well these days — give or take minor items. Of course, by the time we got there we were somewhat over the effects of the stark horrors of Berthoud Pass.

And THEN? Yes, you clever people! THE DONNER

PASS. I can understand how the original Donner party was reduced to cannibalism. At least we were biting each other's heads off before we got through that caper. Nerves?

They're rebuilding it. So you now go on the old road, laid out by slow witted oxen in 1066. Indeed, *before* the invention of the wheel. At the moment it's almost wide enough for two very narrow compact cars to pass one another, with great care.

The drivers of enormous trailer trucks hadn't caught on the day we made it. They flung around those curves with boyish abandon, disregarding the horrible vista below as if God had given them absolute guarantee of safe arrival at their questionable destinations. To them our destinations were inconsequential. For one thing, I suppose, they had all come *from* our destinations and, having seen them, were plunging ahead, waving banners reading "Excelsior."

To divert me, Gladys read aloud the historical note from the AAA guide in which was described how the members of the original party et each other. Then it went right on to say how picnic tables had been put out for us at convenient intervals.

But then the breathtaking west side of the Pass. Sudden greenness. Warmth. Things growing out of the ground, not from pots.

San Francisco is fantastic. And that's the original thought for this week.

Love to all,
Francis

*Dear Friends,*

Behold, we are both accepted at the above for two months! And what a place. Apartment, meals, study, studio, plus an allotment for supplies. I couldn't spend mine in two months of the most furious painting without pulling fasties. We didn't even ask for allotments.

You will be interested in the final road into the Foundation grounds. Rustic Canyon is rustic. And deep. It is our fate! Berthoud, Donner and, as a final kick in our sensitive stomachs, *this.*

About three miles of country road the width of a coffee table, with curves just wide enough for my great ark of a car to manage, very little — and at times *no* protection against a gut-twisting view straight down on the top of what used to be Will Rogers' haven. The first time, as we were coming in, we agreed to turn around, at the first possibility, and go back to Vermont (by the southern route). Well, there wasn't any place to turn around or even breathe deeply. Passing? PASSING? Who ya kidding, Bub? But finally we did get to the bottom, after nearly killing myself on an enormous electric gate which I didn't know was automatic. And I made a record (for me) on that stupid ox path. I threw up only three times. *That* was yesterday.

We both had bad dreams last night (our first night here) and today got up and, looking one another straight in the stomachs, said, "Are we mice or people?" I held out for mice, but courage prevailed and at 10:30 we went back up that road, down to Sunset Boulevard, had a nice chat with Nita Naldi,

Clara Bow and the late John Barrymore, had my brakes tightened and came back again. And I'll be darned if the horror didn't recede. Next time I'm going to drive over that path with one eye shut and spit at times into that vast depth. Just to show someone. Like me.

Actually this is a magnificent place. And working conditions wondrous. This final end of the canyon seems miles from the gaudiness of Los Angeles. It's really only a very few.

However, there are many rattlers (now mostly hibernating) and tarantulas (who ain't! I saw one only yesterday) and other alarming forms of life which make the spine of one who has never seen anything more formidable than a skunk (loose, that is) tingle.

As usual, love to all,
Francis

You will, I hope, be happy to know that things go well with us here in the canyon. That we are about a half-hour's drive from Los Angeles and all its heady nonsense seems silly. We do venture out, once in a while, but are always happy to get back here where serenity reigns and the rule is that no one, under any circumstances save the most urgent (like word of a large inheritance, but nothing under half a million dollars) is allowed to knock on our studio or study door.

At the moment there are fourteen Fellows-in-Residence here. Painters, writers, but no composers — a rare situation, we are told. My studio houses a fine piano which I feel mildly guilty about, but what the hell — I ain't Aaron Copland, I'm *me.* So once in a while I tinkle on it, with slight nostalgia about 118 or 203 South Willard Street. I guess we did miss gathering around one or other of those pianos at Christmas, but spending it with David and Lorrie in Berkeley was wonderful, too. Gladys borrowed a sewing machine and made Lorrie a suit. And, by gravy, was able to keep it secret till Christmas morning. That Gladys! Sometimes it's all I can do to keep from telling her how much I love her!

All four of us trekked to Mill Valley to have Christmas dinner amid the roses clustered around Clement Hurd's hilltop house. Fortunately, Clem met us in the valley and led us up and around the switch-back curves to his door. Of course we got hopelessly lost in Muir Woods on our way home in the dark, but gradually worked our way out of the maze.

Now then, about our well-being. Two-three nights ago another of the Fellows-in-Residence — chap named Martin

Dibner — novelist (*Show Case, Deep Six,* which don't seem to ring a bell in my head) — asked us in for tea (!) at 11 P.M. As a complement to the tea he gave us honest-to-God hardtack. Seems he spent some time in Arctic areas and this hardtack was very well aged. And in case you don't know what that means, Vermont granite is as child's play by comparison. Being a good sort and ever ready for the next frolic, I chomped down on some of the stuff without, alas, dunking it. I assumed it was a sort of mature Ritz cracker with a bit more body to it. Well, as you know, I have had certain mechanical (and totally false) aid, upper-tooth-wise. So I spent half an hour in total silence (some kind of record, I am sure) covering the fact that my bridgework had given.

For a day I increased a reputation for stand-offishness. Smiling to one's fellow Fellows-in-Residence is a major tenet of the local ground rules. And last night we had to have dinner with Our Leader, Dr. John Vincent, Director of Huntington Hartford, composer, recent head of the Music Department at U.C.L.A., along with a special guest, the current head of the U.C.L.A. Art Department. Both learned and formidable types. The latter was fetched as a special goody for me to chew on. You know, exchange of ideas, like, "Tell me, Doctor, what do you do with *your* old turpentine?" So I sat there, saying "yes" and "no" and cursing hardtack. I have likely gone down in his book as a lesser luminary of the Jukes family. However, he was so kind as to ask me over to U.C.L.A. for a tour of inspection of the Art Department and by then I shall be totally in tooth and, patently, more articulate. I trust you are not eating dinner right now.

To continue about things going well: yesterday morning I discovered a flat tire on our C. P. Smith Company Ford. Now, in this canyon one cannot *afford* a flat tire. First, there is a very narrow, winding, and long road out of this situation. And only one — that one. Second, because of recent dry weather the fire threat is alarming. We are not allowed to smoke, even pipes, out of doors. Last year they did have a fire up the canyon, less than a mile away — two mountains totally burned off. The painters here were quite literally sinking their paintings in the swimming pool (except the water colorists, of course). And everyone was evacuated to a Los Angeles hotel for five days. So, with these thoughts flashing through my mind, and thoughtfully running my tongue over my somewhat empty upper gum, I damned well got to work changing that tire. "Francis," I said to myself (I was alone at the time), "make it neat, sure and quick."

This time, need I say, the jack wouldn't fetch the car up *high* enough. I got the old tire off, but the spare wouldn't go *on*. Nor would the *flat* tire go back on, as moral support, in case the car fell over while I stood and thought.

There was no doubt but that a canyon fire (God's wrath) was imminent. My sins, which, alas, are many, came upon me vividly, as one's life passes before him at the hour of death. So I went and got a large piece of wood from a woodshed, thus endangering my already fated life, because who knows where a tarantula lurks in this strange valley? I put it under the tireless wheel, let the jack down, placed a 2 x 4 under the base of the jack (I must patent that idea), raised the car, put the spare tire on, went into town today, had my bridgework mended and only at this very moment realize there has been no canyon fire.

We are happy and busy, which, to be blindingly original, are one and the same, especially if anybody cottons to his work.

Most affectionately,
Francis

———

## Mes Enfants (of all persuasions — even Republicans),

Today the radio announced rain within two days. Well, we will see. This kind of devil-may-care prognostication has been dished up too often for me to put any more faith in it than I do in that other come-on I've been hearing about — that personal income taxes are going down.

It's so *dry* around here that I never pee *in*side when I can do it *out*side, on one of our crackling dry hillsides — hoping God will take the hint and pull THAT CHAIN.

We have had day after golden day of miraculous sunshine, which has been, to Gladys and me, like finding a *real* diamond ring in *every* box of Wheaties. (In Vermont, in January, you're lucky to find even Wheaties in a box of Wheaties.)

Well, the last few days have been overcast and we eye the sky with interest and hope. Thus far the overcast has turned out to be a combination of celestial kidding and smog. But today the muck up above really looks like clouds and the radio boys are more positive.

Things here, of course, come either black or white. The Californian Mother Nature, we are told, is a first class witch, who has a special loathing for human beings. She denies you any liquid sustenance for months and then, like a sow with a hundred and one teats, squirts all over you, to the point of inundation.

There is an arroyo (creek to you, kids) which meanders through our canyon. Right now it is as dry as a Neanderthal's bones. Last January it overflew its banks and deposited four inches of revolting crud on the floors of three of our studios.

Like I say, nobody has any taste in or even near Los Angeles. Even Mother Nature. Now if I had that many teats — oh, well. I haven't.

Last week someone discovered that neither Gladys nor I had ever been submitted to the physical examination required of all Fellows-in-Residence on these hallowed grounds. I suspect they worry mostly about social diseases which, I increasingly realize, means, hereabouts, a familiarity with such dirty phrases as "trade union." So, somewhat belatedly, we were sent into town to a doctor "of the Foundation's choice." Amongst other odd facts about us, he discovered that Gladys had wax in her ears, a problem which he dispatched with some skill. He is, I am sure, still frustrated by the bats which he found in my belfry. Only a high priest can exorcise them. He did, however, tell me that I can never be a mother again. Natural or otherwise.

But if *Somebody* doesn't give with the water over this parched area pretty soon there will be hell to pay. We have one Fellow who constantly scares the wits out of all of us, even himself! He is a chain smoker — a brilliant and pathetically unhappy guy, doing a book on Conrad, being himself a Pole. We all ask him over, in a sort of rotating system, after dinner, to give black coffee and talk, hoping he will thereafter go to bed.

The problem is that he gets crocked about once a week. And when he does he walks all the long way, over this tinder-dry canyon road, to Santa Monica for, alas, a few more — chain smoking all the way and doubtless letting live cigarette butts fall where they may. It's enough to make your public hairs stand on end. One live cigarette in the wrong place and we will have had it. Up a well-known creek, without whatever it is you use in a dry creek in lieu of a paddle.

Our work seems to go well. Gladys labors on stories, a

new and, I suspect, exciting and challenging medium for her, but also continues to produce poems which seem to me remarkably fine. I paint in a new world, drawing my notions (as I guess I must) from my immediate surroundings. The evaluation of what I am up to will have to come later and thousands of miles from here. I don't know yet how well my digestion of this unfamiliar fare is working. Gladys is a wonder, wherever she is.

Thank you for your good letter.

Love to all,
Francis

Where is a letter giving information about Burlington, Vermont? Won't anyone of you *write,* or at least send us an interesting copy of the *Free Press*? Or are the copies as dull as usual?

Our life goes on in a well-regulated manner, with much work and frequent evening socials at which we quilt, bob for apples and get to know our other Fellows-in-Residence. And, oddly enough, we always seem to be home at ten o'clock.

At the moment we are fifteen — all painters or writers — and every writer is "doing," as they put it, "a Novel." Gladys is the only poet and *she* is also working on short stories. Prose is catching. Next week, however, composer Douglas Moore arrives. Most recent arrival is a nervous chap named Tony Tuttle, who turns out to be a friend of Clair Leonard.

The political complexion amongst us runs from Birch almost to Marx, making for odd table talk at times. I am temporarily and rather annoyingly befriended by a fat old painter from San Francisco whose work, talk, thought and person constitute one *shattering* cliché. He insists on taking me, next Friday, to the luncheon meeting of the Los Angeles Rotary Club! One of his art world heroes is Maxfield Parrish. How *he* ever got here I don't know, save that he is a friend of Huntington Hartford who is himself not noted for his liberalism.

Incidentally, we are told there is some suspicion of all the inmates here. We learned of it at first hand today. As we came back from town, at the entrance to our haven we were met by a group of lads about eight or ten years old. The more courageous stepped forward and said, "Are you really albinos?"

I quickly looked at the top of my head and said, "Why, yes, we are, and we all come from ALBINIA."

Amongst our favorite folk are Paul and Nina Chavchavadze. We knew them for quite a spell before we came upon Paul's book called *Family Album*. She is vaguely working on memoirs. She is a person of about sixty-two-three who approaches a topic of conversation from all points of the compass at one and the same time, flitting like a deranged bird from one to another all the while, then suddenly she swoops down on the very fact and truth and essence of the issue with breathtaking precision. She's a livin' wonder!

When I first saw that ugly-handsome face a very faint bell tinkled. I had *seen* that face, somewhere. Like in picture books.

Well, Paul's book revealed all. I'll be darned if she isn't the first (genuine) member of a royal family I've ever met. Her maiden name was Romanov. Her father was the Grand Duke George, her grandfather was the Grand Duke Michael, brother of Alexander II, and her great grandfather was Nicholas I — "Tsar," as they used to say, "of all the Russias." And with a beard she'd be the spit and image! Her mother was Princess Marie of Greece, and her maternal grandparents were King George and Queen Olga of same. The current George of Greece is thus her cousin and, she explains, "duller than yesterday's dishwater." I delight in her because of my intense interest in tangible history. (Remember that I went all the way to Springfield, Illinois to stand on the *same* front stoop Lincoln stood on.) She never mentions her past — we never would have known had we not read Paul's book — but she is generous to me with her memories because she knows about this *thing* I have about history you can reach out and *touch*. She knows I have no great admiration for some of her family, but as a living link with a long-gone world, she overwhelms me. How screwy can my sense of nostalgia get?

Paul is tall, handsome, a prince of the Stroganoff clan and knows more dirty limericks than even I do. Paul's book is light and good for a rainy night. (Houghton Mifflin, 1949, in case anyone is interested.)

I have finally conquered the ROAD. And the local wild life (another of my initial alarms) is thus far benign. No snakes, no more tarantulas after that first one — which leaves only raccoons immediately about. *They* come to our door almost every night for handouts. Knowing that most writers and painters are, themselves, usually in touch-and-go straits, the raccoons have adopted a "let's share the poverty" line and actually thump on the screen door until we go out and give them such goodies as crusts and used shoe laces. They eat out of our hands, never removing more than one finger at a time. Thoughtful little beasts and *very* cute. Unfortunately, they know it. There must be thousands in this canyon. There are also coyotes, foxes, and, further up the canyon, three dinosaurs named Agnes, Mabel and Becky. We have not seen any of these as yet. I did, however, see the discarded skin of one of them on the road yesterday. It had shrunk some.

You may be shocked to know that neither Gladys nor I ever learned to play poker until last night, when Our Leader, Dr. John Vincent, and his daughter (girls' school senior) began teaching us. Since I have a very poor memory and can't count beyond twenty (that being when I run out of fingers and toes), I promise to be a most inept pupil. Gladys, however, who, as you know, has more fingers and toes than *I* do, nearly cleaned up the joint. We are going home by way of Las Vegas where I shall set her up long enough to win money for the trek East.

Last night we got word that David and Lorrie are safely

in Burlington. How they ever made it in their 1952 Plymouth is a mystery. That parody of a car drank (and threw out) oil the way Barbara Hutton drank (and threw out husbands).

Our love to all,
Francis

So you want to know about *flora,* do you? Believe me, kid, we've got it out here. Including a few varieties unknown south of Nome, Alaska, and at least two never seen north of Mexico City, Mexico (pop. 2,235,000). I don't know the pop. of Nome, Alaska, but assume it to be less.

To begin with, flora-wise, California is in a *state* (get it?) of idiotic hysteria. Outside our door grow a number of orange trees. Yesterday I picked two ripe oranges from one of them whilst Gladys was picking orange *blossoms* from the same tree. Things are better ordered in Vermont. When Tiny Long goes out into his orchard, come autumn, and starts picking apples from a tree of his'n, his wife hardly expects to go picking apple blossoms from the same tree, does she? Mother California is like those monstrous females you read about every now and then who get leather medals from the Pope for having given birth to triplets every four months for twelve years running. To say California is fecund is to say Niagara is damp.

Ah, yes — flora! We run into strange and challenging flora here. It's a hell of a lot better *not* to run into some kinds, they say, without a rope around your waist and a trusted friend holding the other end. Outside our door, hanging from one of those unlikely sycamore trees, is an ominously luxuriant vine which Gladys keeps snipping and potting. Why? I worry. Do I begin to bore her? Let's face it, old friend. There is more than *one kind* of ivy. That's what she says it is — a kind of ivy. Each morning I notice that vine is hovering right over the car, un- dulating — just *undulating.* Obviously, during the night, it has crept into the car, through *closed* windows, and has turned on the parking lights which I am *sure* I turned off the night before. Furthermore, it gets into the house, steals the car keys, and deposits them in the ignition switch. It all seems odd.

"Back East," as so many of us say here nostalgically, we have something called fuchsia. Like most well-bred, St. Paul's-Harvard type flowers, it blooms once a year. Often around New Year's Eve. Well, we saw one here not two days ago and started to pick it. As our hands approached, it *growled* at us. Almost too late we learned that its local name is *re*fuchsia.

I referred, shortly back, to *vine*. A rather special California blossom, indigenous to Hollywood and Vine, is the frizzled frump, known also as the night-blooming, or darkling, tart. Its native color is puce but, like a chameleon, it changes color according to circumstance. And believe me, sweetheart, circumstances at Hollywood and Vine change almost as fast as the Dow-Jones average.

I am only trying to help you, so I'm giving it straight. Take the periwrinkle. This is found, too, near Hollywood and Vine, but usually on side streets. It's an older type flower — mildly wrinkled — having bloomed some twenty years back, but still valiantly thrusting up shoots — or, as we say here, "feelers" — but with its roots firmly sunk into precisely the same kind of stuff from which the newer growths spring. West or East, fertilizer is basically the same.

Goodness, there are so many types! The fringed purple gusset, for example, which inserts itself between other growths. And the false grudge. There is a fine example of the latter right here on the Foundation grounds. We all feel the son-of-a-bitch should be cut down, but, as I have indicated, some of these things bite back, so we try to keep our distance.

A rather *nice* event is the sudden appearance of two delightful examples of the early (or spring) cowlick. They didn't actually appear on the same day, but very soon discovered their affinity. Interested as we are in growing things, we occasionally remove them to the oceanside, for watering. We almost feel like parents.

You will forgive one allusion to *fauna*. Last night, driving in from Santa Monica (we had just been to Santa Monica), we spotted a fox. Quickly looking at our watches, we realized it was a 20th Century Fox. (The watches out here show that sort of thing — if you see what I mean. I'm sure I don't.)

The only other note on *flora* I can report concerns a large plant right outside the door of the Community House. It is a multi-colored monstrosity which, I am told, eats people. I am fascinated by it and have approached to within three feet. I have *seen* it eat flies and bees. Come to think of it, this morning, as I was shaving, I noticed in the mirror that I wasn't *there*.

You will *love* California.

The other evening we had the great delight of hearing a superb recording of *The Ballad of Baby Doe* (New York City Opera job — Beverly Sills, Walter Cassel, Frances Bible et al.). About ten of us foregathered with Douglas Moore who wrote the music. He gave us a wonderful fill-in on the action before each scene. A fine opera. At the end of the last scene I damned near had to flee the room for fear of showing my emotions. I noted that Douglas was himself quite casually crying. He seems, incidentally, to have set himself the task of selling me opera. If he is successful, maybe my friends will have more respect for my musical taste when we return.

(If, of course, they ever get me out of this man-eating plant. It's nice in here, but the odor is close and sweet.)

Love to all,
Francis

Behold, *rain* has come! Gentle, long lasting rain. This is the first rain our area has had in three hundred and twenty days. And that, for once, is *not* a Chamber of Commerce figure. Do you wonder we lie awake nights, thinking every dry leaf blowing over the drive is the distant crackle of an all-consuming fire?

The thing is we don't have single leaves blowing over our road, but thousands. Large, brittle ones from these special California sycamore trees which aren't the simple, homey sycamores of the benign East. These are large and tortuous parodies of sane, self-contained trees. The leaves grow beyond imagination, covering, in some cases, not merely the span of a large outstretched hand, but that of a seated behind. At night they scratch and complain over this hard-surfaced drive like the claws of death, at the slightest stirring of the wind. *One* of these leaves, off on a wind-born journey, can give you the jitters. *Lots* of them, all sounding off at once, add up to a death rattle. We have lived with this sound for thirty days and (especially) nights.

So comes this blessed rain. The leaves are sodden. They lie in heaps, wilted and harmless and bereft of their idiotic power of suggestion, no longer symbols of imminent horror — but a bunch of lousy wet leaves which annoy us because I have to park my car right in the middle of a great batch of them. Carefully deposited precisely *there* by a malignantly predisposed THING.

Honest, kids, I love this place. It loves *me,* too, in its backhanded way. It's simply a matter of defining terms — of coming to an understanding.

Two days ago Gladys and I went out over the precipitous canyon road, it being almost totally obliterated by fog and needlepoint rain — only to confront a special testimony of Southern California's affection. As we rounded the most horrifying curve on this, at best, thought-provoking road, a whole bunch of rocks hurtled down in front of the car as if to say, "O.K., you Eastern Punk, show your credentials." It seems that when it rains here we have landslides. Nobody warned me about *that* in Hardwick, Vermont. They pass it off here, in the depth of the canyon, as they pass off so many other things — love, snakes, tarantulas, life, birth, scorpions, marriage, divorce, poison oak and oranges on *trees*. (I still think someone went out to the Grand Union, *bought* those oranges and stitched them onto the trees, just out our windows, to practical-joke Gladys and me. How far can they go? Next they'll be telling us *olives* come on trees instead of in martinis.)

Last night we celebrated Gladys' birthday. Like me, she has turned thirty. A modest gathering of folk. To our startled delight Dr. Vincent and his wife appeared. We are told they never do this sort of thing. *She* drank a whole jelly tumbler full of Bourbon and then half another. *He* reminisced delightfully about musical events and people.

Paul Chavchavadze, husband of the astonishing Nina, has become obsessed with the notion that Gladys *loves* tequila and fetched her a bottle. The poor girl actually *hates* it, but stoically sat here taking modest sips. We finally got clever and fed most of it to him!

Me, I kept lighting my pipe with frail matches from a strange new box thereof, breaking one after another and cursing them roundly. And, alas, audibly. Seems they were a rather special gift to Gladys from Vincent's secretary who was sitting next to me. She is deaf. I hope she is deaf *enough*.

One strange problem has finally been clarified. For some time now we both have been having a queer sense of being (a) near a moment from childhood and (b) near a Vicks Vapo-Rub factory. With the rain bringing out certain local odors in full pungency, we have solved it! By gravy, it's the eucalyptus trees.

Neither of us can remember *any* ointment, salve, unguent or exterior body pacifier from early life that didn't have this unique smell. Eucalyptus oil, of course! It was in everything. From a distance it is one of the most nostalgic scents I know. Close, after rain, it has, alas, the smell of sewer gas. It's like lampreys. One or two, yes. But a surfeit — and, sweet Mary, there goes your ball game!

Today is Sunday, which I recognize as such only when I notice, at breakfast, that Walter Sorge (a fine Canadian painter) is wearing a *necktie.* That means he is going to church. The rest of us seem to work right through Sunday, but Walter's Sunday tie gives us pause. I suspect we all go to our studios and praise God in our private ways.

This afternoon Walter, Gladys and I decided we would do well to quit the cloister for a spell on other than churchly matters and sallied forth in my trusty Ford station-wagon — body color, white — motor no. 02 64W 135818 — color of hair, questionable — color of eyes, pink (see recent letter concerning albinos). We called on a friend of Walter's, about twenty-five miles up the four-lane pike called Route 101. Had a long and pleasant walk up the friend's ranch canyon. We saw many deer tracks and were surrounded by foliage obviously invented by a mad botanist from a figment of the imagination called Southern California.

Then on to other friends of Walter who, as one might have known from the Sunday morning tie bit, were entertaining missionaries from the Far East. And from where I sit I don't mean Boston, Mass. These final hosts live in circumstances which beggar description. The house is high above the Pacific, five miles north of Malibu Beach, itself a tourist horror. After the rain, this became *the* day for testing the old notion that "every prospect pleases and only man is vile." The vileness of man was evident about six hundred feet below us on Route 101. Cars, trucks, motorcycles, scooters, bicycles, buses, people on horses and even afoot, all in a mad rat race to see who would get into or out of Los Angeles first, the winner in either case getting a free funeral, with modest floral tributes.

The prospect that pleased lay some rods to the west, and we were looking down on it, too. There the Pacific came rolling in from Hawaii and Japan, in long, deliberate, majestic and impersonal rolls, breaking on the beaches in the kind of soap suds thunder that makes Little Hosmer seem sort of puny. (Not that I ain't still loyal.) It grabbed me where I live. We could see fifteen miles, both left and right, and almost hear everyone of those enormous breakers roar.

Our timing, coming home, got screwed. The final stretch (seven miles) took us forty-five minutes. Foreigners from California kept getting in my way.

So tomorrow I must work twice as hard to make up for today's giddy venture into the outside world.

Love still,
Francis

---

I feel it incumbent upon me to send final intelligence from this quarter of the battlefield before we retreat, on March 4, in a south-easterly direction — our rears guarded by a stack of pictures, some of David's furniture, and a few cases of sartorial ammunition.

As for David's furniture, I am attached to it. These two chairs and one table constitute the very first stuff he and Lorrie bought for their apartment during their initial connubial bliss. Like idiots, we agreed to fetch it all back East for them. We stowed these three pieces in our car in Berkeley, unloaded them here and will shortly load them *in* again. Whilst here they have been part of our local decor. Like I say, I have become *attached.* Only last night I spent twenty minutes getting my pants *un*-attached from a broken strand of bamboo or raffia or seaweed or whatever it is they make these bamboo or raffia or seaweed things out of. David and Lorrie should have been *more* attached already! I got my own problems.

In the meantime, I offer a final report on *flora* and *fauna.* First, *flora.* Five days ago the sycamore trees around here were starkly naked. All the enormous, dry, rattling leaves had fallen to earth, to scurry back and forth at night under our windows, making noises like doom.

Today, six (6) days later, our 80° weather has produced a miracle. *New* leaves have appeared which, in these few days, have grown to the maximum size of any maple leaf that ever took a chance on Vermont's fortuitous weather. Suddenly this deep valley and its surrounding hills are a riot of green. Flowers bloom over night. Oranges, like ripe virgins, beg to be plucked and squeezed. The poison oak is rampant. We have three lovely vases of it, right in this room, which Gladys unfortunately confused with trailing arbutus. Her left hand has more or less *gone*, up to the elbow, but her *right* hand is still intact. Thank God she's right-handed (except in her compliments). We'll have to *make do* until she grows another left hand, but in this climate we figure two weeks will do it.

As to *fauna* —
Three days ago I went in to the very *heart* of Los Angeles — Pershing Square — (named, obviously, in a moment of national hysteria) and was back *here* in less than half an hour. Meanwhile, a mountain lion had been seen within fifty feet of *our* front door.

And last night, as I was right in the *middle* of a mouthful of *eel*, my dinner-mate announced he had just killed the first rattlesnake of the season on an open and previously benign road. After friends had revived us with smelling salts, Gladys and I went up to view the remains. They were large, ugly and still twitching. "Hell," said a member of the coroner's staff, "that's a small one!"

We are happy to be leaving this lovely spot. It has been voted the very *best* picnic the club has had this year. (The only dissenting votes came from the little Colburn kids who, despite being on their honeymoon — and they do make a cute couple — don't like snakes.)

Two days previous, an hypnotically handsome little snake — striped, as I am now sitting, from north to south — was come upon in the laundry room, put into a Hellman's Mayonnaise jar — empty, that is — and exhibited. They called it a coral king snake. A harmless little thing that near broke the jar, striking again and again at my finger.

Days later

Well, well, here we are in Texas! Not a bad state, as Texaci go. We have been driving in it for eighteen days now, looking for the Louisiana border. Thus far no one we have met has ever *heard* of Louisiana, but Gladys is convinced it lies in an easterly direction and that we must persevere. "Texas," she keeps saying, "was not built in a day." I agree. Not God Himself could have turned out all *this* stuff in a day. Last night, after a particularly hard bout with the horses, cattle and women, we found a water hole, a place to bed down and, oddly enough, a rather plush restaurant for dinner.

We ordered two glasses of Red Eye whiskey and I retired to the available conveniences. After tidying up in what seemed to me rather nicely scented quarters, I emerged. I was greeted, to my delight, with nods and becks and even wreathed smiles — all aimed in my direction. I poised on that threshold for a moment, realizing that of course all those *other* customers had recognized me as the creator of *A Graduation Address*, not to mention "Landscape #3" and "Landscape #4." Graciously bowing from left to right, amidst demonstrations of appreciation, which at times approached outright sniggering, I resumed my seat. Spoilsport Gladys quietly pointed to the door from which I had just emerged, on which was printed in large, black and unmistakable letters: LADIES.

I may possibly be the *only* man in Texas' long and glorious history who ever took a leak in the ladies' room. Oh, well, someone has to break the ice. Departmentalization is the curse of our age. We all pea in the same pod — or *something* like that.

Even *later*

Behold, we are in New Orleans, in a very fancy hostelry called the *Oh You Kid Motel*. I know it is exclusive because the manageress (or "madam," as they are locally called) tells me so.

She is a delightful, motherly type who affects a local get-up of artificially blond hair, a sort of house coat or dressing gown, and rather *heavy* facial make-up — considering the temperature. She is fat and jolly and currently has lots of young *girls* as guests, too. As she explains, the Louisiana Girl Guides are having their yearly camp-out this week. Lots of men are around, too, going and coming, going and coming, as men will.

We have spent a great deal of time in the French Quarter, or the Vieux Carré, as the local foreigners call it. I bought a beret made, it says right *on* it, in Paris, France. Gladys bought two post cards, one of the Washington Monument and the other of the Capitol Building in Montpelier, Vermont. Also a half-pound of peanut brittle as a sort of memorial gesture to Robert E. Lee. As you may know, he is famous in these parts for having won the recent War-between-the-States. Except at the end.

Lots later

We are in either Columbus, Georgia; Columbia, South Carolina; Columbus, Ohio; or Washington, District of Columbia. It is raining very hard, all the rivers are *over* their banks, and the vision from this window is so watery that I suspect we are actually in Columbia, the Gem of the *Ocean*.

*Whatever* it is, it is named after that great Pilgrim Father, Christopher Columbus, who, along with Ethan Allen, Zane Grey and Lydia E. Pinkham, helped founder these United States. (To name only a few.)

*Somewhere* along our way I have had the pleasure of putting my finger on the very *pulse* of the Civil War. It seems

General Sherman marched to the sea, laying, every now and then, Waste.

    In one of these Columbus or Columbia type state capitals stands the capitol *building*, with still visible dents made by Sherman's artillery boys. One of these, family saga has it, was my great uncle, Ogden Read. He is reputed to have layed more than mere Waste en route.

Oh God — later still!

We are in Washington, D.C. John Kennedy has been tied up, as have been Senators Aiken and Prouty. Also Congressman Stafford and the doorman at the Mayflower Hotel. We were, however, able to squeeze in a moment for columnist Vonda Bergman.

    Tomorrow we head for Albany, New York and, since nobody in his right mind has anything new or good to say about Albany, New York (unless he wants to be President), I close this, my final message, with these words:

    "Love to all,"
    Francis

The time has come to set pen to paper. I've had three seizures of this kind before, but recovered sufficiently never to go through with any of them. We are in Paris (France, that is) after heady times in Italy. On Tuesday, April 23, 1963, we leave for Liège to visit our AFS son, Pol de Waleffe. We called from here yesterday, confirming our date of arrival. Since I am not noted for my fluency in any language save Vermontese, Gladys done all the talking. She got Pol's *mother* who knows no English, but was so excited at our imminent arrival that she couldn't *stop* talking. It was all very cordial and lively, with Gladys saying "oui" constantly. Neither of us has the slightest idea *what* that conversation was all about, but assume that sometime during April we will see Pol. In the meantime, I have stopped eating in Paris, anticipating the phone bill.

So from Liège to London, by way of numerous Belgium cities loaded with feasts of Brueghel, etc., to Montreal to Burlington to Craftsbury (Vermont, of course) at some date in early May convenient to Alitalia. Alas, we had to give up Greece because of *time* and, of course, *money.* But we are so full of *ancient* things seen in Italy that it may suffice. Old marble is coming out our ears. Only this morning Gladys, on some girlish whim, called me "old Marble head." Since she has forgotten half *she* saw in Italy, I got even with her by subtly pointing out that she seemed to be *without* some of her marbles (phrase I coined "on the spot" — or, as the French have it, the *prix fixe*). By the way, don't try to pronounce *that* phrase unless you know French. You might get into trouble with the waitress.

There are so many things to say about Italy, many of them nice! We arrived in Roma upright and were met by Charlie Keller, an old friend who, with kindly wife, took us in for the night. The next day we rented a room on the Piazza Navona, in the apartment of Karl Kraber whom we once knew as a kid in Southern Vermont and who is now one of the best known flautists in Europe — honest! Another phrase I coined in connection with *this* turn of events is "it's a small world, ain't it?" Likely to catch on, I feel. After a week in Roma, turning over old stones for the Italian government in the interests of antiquity, and repairing some of the older church frescoes (as a gesture of international good will), the Colburns and Kellers headed for Firenze by car. Despite the fact that Charlie drives about 90 miles an hour (*miles*, not kilometers) and the road from Roma to Firenze is narrow, often very high up, and enhanced with some of the most breathtaking hairpins it has ever been my horror to excrete on, we *got* there.

Charlie's wife is an ardent student of Italian painting and we couldn't have had a better guide. We stayed for five days, heading out each morning to rape the treasures of the Palazzo Vecchio, Santa Maria del Fiore, Santa Croce, Santa Maria Novella, the Uffizi, the Pitti — on and on. It is rather sobering to stand on the very spot where Savonarola was burned, and to see, in San Marco, his tiny cell, his beads, his haircloth shirt, the books he *handled* — and the astonishing portrait of him by Fra Bartolomeo. (Again, this *thing* I have about the *real* stuff, not the expert replica!) Florence is so rich as to humble the haughtiest scholar. Me, simple soul that I am, almost got religion there. Please, *please* go to the monastery of San Marco and sit a long time before Fra Angelico's "Adoration." I finally had to leave for the simple reason that my tears were too evident. These fellows painted *good*.

Back in Roma, I put my mind seriously to the matters of (1) Italian coinage and (2) a few handy phrases. The first came hard since even American money confounds me. In Roma the nuances of buying a cup of coffee and a biscuit are manifold. You often pay *one* person for the coffee and *another* for the biscuit. I shall never forget how I disrupted one establishment by walking in, at 10:00 A.M., and ordering and (I *thought*) paying for coffee and biscuit. Seems I paid the wrong people for the wrong things. Finally, at 4:00 P.M., they closed the joint down and called in a public accountant. Like I said in another connection, it cements international relations. Ten years from now I will still be a myth amongst Italian restaurateurs. My *spoken* Italian has contributed considerably. A typical reason involves the day I finally screwed up my courage and went, all alone, to a small coffee bar, having for hours before practiced this sentence: "Cappuccino con zucchero, per piacere." When I confronted the waiter, all courage fled, a state of total confusion set in, and I said something which, I am told, translates roughly as follows: "Capistrano, you sucker, and peace — peace." As I say, they'll not soon forget old Frank Colburn in Roma.

The area around the Piazza Navona is ancient. The Piazza, once a chariot race-course, now studded with three gorgeous fountains sculpted by Bernini, was directly outside our window. The house we lived in was built shortly before Columbus sailed to discover us. This, of course, is all rather recent for Roma. The plumbing, by the way, is apparently the original. But these Romans rarely use plumbing.

In heaven's name, don't try to *drive* in Roma! Save for a few major thoroughfares, the streets are about half as wide as the road over Eden Mountain and you walk single file on the one and a half foot side walks (if any exist) or get killed. Traffic is fantastically dense on these little paths and a conservative speed is about 70 m.p.h. The millions of scooters, of course, go much faster. The philosophy is, "He who chickens first chickens first, and his name shall be chicken."

Food? Very good, but rather heavy. Wine? Good, but oh, these French! Tonight, here in Paris, I pinched our waitress. She pinched me back. So did Gladys. So did the proprietor. *That* much for French wine.

Our last day in Roma offered a rather unexpected climax. We went *back* to the Vatican, for reasons of *art,* to be confronted, to our astonishment, by Pope John, who *blessed* us! Seems we walked in on his usual Wednesday public audience. I feel about as I did before, but it's pretty thrilling to *see* and *hear* one of the wisest and most courageous popes in history. And if you don't believe *that*, read his last encyclical. It ain't papal bull. It's a tragedy for the world that he is a very old and very sick man.

A final word on Roma. Watch out for doggie-does. No one curbs his dog there. No curbs. Dogs move wherever they are moved to move.

Like one-two before us, we are totally in love with Paris. We get along well with the language. The only problem is this damned business of the *old* and *new* franc. The old ones are still extant — coin and paper — and look deceptively like the new ones. To be confronted by *this*, to one who is still trying to comprehend the Italian lira, is unnerving. I hope the American dollar is still worth 19¢ (or is it 20¢?) when we get home.

One event concerning the French language unhinges our faith in a small paper-back called *French for Your Travels — Phrase Book and Pocket Dictionary,* put out by the Berlitz boys. It came about this way: in a restaurant in Paris, not twenty-four hours ago, we saw three obviously American ladies, of a certain age, all holding their *noses* and saying "Non!" whilst a perplexed waiter was offering them some cheese. It seemed rude of them. One held this little booklet in her hand. Having the booklet on *my* person, I idly thumbed through it, to come upon *this*, quoted here in full (see page 13 of book): "French has a tricky nasal pronunciation which we have represented by 'ng' at the end of the word, as in *un* (uhng). This sound can best be attained by holding your nose as you say it."

Oh, well. May I close by mentioning European toilet paper? It's either No. 00 *sand*paper or an odd form of *waxed* paper, unfamiliar to me. In either case, it's non-absorbent. *Pat*, they tell me, don't *rub*! Nuts! *The New York Times* is better any day in the week, especially Sunday. *That* lasts *all* week!

Love,
Franny

P.S. Forgot to mention delightful cocktail party at the home of the director of The American Academy in Rome. A veritable (and *old*) palace, complete with servants. About ten folk, all delightful. And dinners with Darius Milhaud's son, in Florence. Painter and mad pixie type. Saw much of him. Went to school in U.S. Mentioned him before.

*My dear children,*

To continue: we are in Liège. Our adopted son, Pol, is now a doctor. And thank God for that! What is called "la malade Americaine," which I am sure I don't need to describe, has finally caught up with me. Every now and again Pol gives me two mysterious pills and two large spoons of dry charcoal impregnated with a secret Belgian nostrum based, possibly, on religious faith. I couldn't dream of blasting Pol's career at its very inception by telling him the stuff don't work. Like the good Vermonter I am, with Calvin Coolidge's example constantly before me, I pucker up and make do. Actually, I exaggerate. I *am* grateful Pol is a doctor. *Someone* has to sign my death certificate.

The hospitality here is *incroyable*! We are not even allowed to spit for ourselves. Pol got a great deal of time off from his hospital duties to show us (we expected) around Liège. We underestimated. Pol and his father met us at the airport in Brussels, about sixty miles from Liège! We had expected to go from Brussels to Liège by train. *Papa* is a gem who assumes my diffidence about French is an affectation of modesty and gives me long lectures on Belgian economy in Rapid Gibberish, the local tongue. Every day a tour is planned for us, to fabulous places — glass works (where all the goblets and stuff for every court and embassy in the world are made) — "views" — but mostly museums and churches.

Day before yesterday Pol headed out with us for a modest little tour of the country-side. His mother, also a gem, had packed a lunch of much fruit and *twenty* sandwiches. And don't underestimate a Belgian sandwich. Each one is a long, fat roll, equal to half a loaf of American bread, full of ham, cheese, etc. We headed out at 8 A.M. and before returning to Liège had pretty thoroughly inspected Antwerp, Spa, Ghent, Brussels, Bruges and the Ardennes. It's a little like taking a day off to visit New York City, Washington, D.C., Boston, Mass., Hardwick, Vt., and then returning to Cleveland, Ohio where you started out.

The reason all this was possible is hinted at in the AAA *Travel Guide to Europe*, page 120. I quote: "There are no speed limits in Belgium. Pedestrians who wish to see the *rest* of Europe should take special heed. One contends with Belgium's individualistic drivers." I now unquote. But add this sobering thought: *no driver's license* is required in Belgium!

Well, Pol is an individualistic driver, albeit *good.* It seems our fate to drive with individualistic operators. Pol's car (Dauphine) was recently caved in on one side by Papa whose driving is a masterpiece of pure invention. So Pol's car's headlights are totally askew. You can't see a thing ahead at night. But Pol's plodding 75 m.p.h. never diminishes, day or night, city corner or country cow path, vision or no vision. As we approached Liège, homeward bound, in, of course, total darkness, I said in jest (and a very weak voice, indeed), "Haven't we got time for Moscow before bed-time?" And Pol said without smiling, "You would really like?" Anyway, yesterday's little trip of quite a few hundred miles, through exquisite picture-book landscapes and small towns, with stops in above-mentioned cities, was wondrous.

If I keep falling in love so often, I shall begin to question my stability. First, *parts* of Rome; then Florence, in toto, but especially Fra Angelico; then Paris, almost in toto, where "Mona Lisa" considerably humbled me by showing how stupid it is to form opinions from *reproductions*. This unexpectedly small and dark picture is pure magic. Well, then Liège, which is actually not very interesting and with which I am only mildly in love; next, Antwerp (wonderful) and Ghent, a real heady affair, but BRUGES! Dear God! Small, sweet, perfect Bruges! I never knew what love was, before. It's idiotic to *describe* Bruges. Just *go* there and stop asking your father all these silly questions. It's like the first flower in spring. It's like your first girl, or inheriting a million dollars from a forgotten uncle by the name of Jan. Like in Jan Van Eyck. We have seen Van Eycks, Memlings, Breughels, and others which curl your toes up and make you lose your breath. Kiddies, from Bruges alone I have inherited more than I can ever spend — even squandering. I wish it had happened earlier. Love, as the feller says, is a funny thing.

To say Bruges is the Venice of the North (and they *do*) is to say Bruges is the Venice of the North, and it don't prove nothing to me. *Venice is the Bruges of the South.* So there.

Today morning we visited the big local museum with a very young university student who lives with the de Waleffes. He knows five languages, comes from Luxemburg and wants to practice his English. He speaks it fairly well, and with *chilling* formality. Before each picture I was given a detailed description of what was before my eyes. (Many Europeans assume Americans (1) know absolutely *nothing* and (2) are blind.) Particularly notable was the moment we confronted an "Expulsion from the Garden of Eden." Assuming the Bible is unknown in America, this young man said, "You know the Bible —no!" And then told the whole story, with lengthy explanations of just *who* Adam and Eve were so I wouldn't miss the *point* of the painting. Finally I gave up and settled on correcting his pronunciation.

In the afternoon Pol and his banker brother drove us to a few other local sights. At one point we reached the highest hill (Liège is in a considerable valley, on the lovely River Meuse) whereon is a famous fortification which, in Belgium's sad recent history, was quite useless. (Forts were out of style when the Germans last visited here.) There are many open courtyards. In one of these, no larger than your living room, I saw the still standing posts to which hundreds of captured Resistance fighters were tied and then shot. I saw the logs piled up immediately in back, to catch occasional misdirected bullets. And just outside, the graves — many, the graves of young boys. Despite birds overhead and children, out beyond, it is the quietest place I have ever been in. I wasn't much good for sightseeing after we left.

At dinner last night was a Resistance fighter who *wasn't* caught. He helped many downed American airmen on their secret way from the Ardennes area back to England. His special delight was feeding them *fresh* vegetables and real (not powdered) eggs. He told of one American to whom he fed *thirteen* fried eggs, in succession, before he realized the American had long since said "enough" — not "un oeuf."

Monday to London. Meanwhile, the usual love to the usual people and any strays who happen to be around. Especially anyone in the car-selling business. Next to crossing the Atlantic, buying a car in Burlington begins to loom as a major problem.

Francis

Behold, we are back. And I mean really back. Craftsbury.

The flight over the Atlantic was uneventful, but when we touched down at Montreal at 11:00 in the morning, we found that planes to Burlington had been cancelled. No transportation until 8:00 in the evening.

We were pooped and took refuge in a movie house where we hoped to sleep, then have a leisurely dinner and board a bus for home. But our queer luck maintained itself. The movie we innocently walked into was Alfred Hitchcock's *The Birds.* Not calculated to induce sleep. In fact, almost as terrifying as some of those passes we navigated in the West. Well, we finally staggered out dazed, then dined and at last arrived in Burlington upright. David and his wife gave us a warm welcome and now here we are in Craftsbury.

We have never before been here so early in spring and find snowbanks on the north side of all the buildings, including ours. Too bad we don't have some maple syrup. We could have sugar on snow.

The lake was still covered with ice when we got here. We had the delight of watching it break up. The water is now open and the May flies are beginning to come out, resulting in hungry birds swooping down in great numbers. We are both startled into reminiscence of Hitchcock and hardly sleep a wink at night.

The people hereabout seem to remember us. The postmaster hands us our mail and visits about local folk with no reservations.

We remain eternally grateful to all of you for a pleasant year's sabbatical and hope to repeat it once again.

Run over and see *us* sometime.

Lovingly,
Francis

# II. "Oh, Francis!"

## A Travelogue

Mr. Chairman and brother members of the Men's Club of Seton's Falls: I am happy and honored that you asked me to talk to you at this first supper meeting of the year which, as you can see, is also our annual Ladies' Night.

And a good thing, too. Them cakes the ladies fetched added considerable to the repast. Not that I ever et one before with purple frosting. As a matter of fact, it's the one Mother whipped up, and when she was putting it in the box I says to her, "Where'd you ever see *purple* frosting on a cake?" And she answered, "Well, Nosey, it *ain't* purple. It's sort of a dark puce." I won't repeat my reply to that one.

Now I presume you want to hear about us folks driving out to California — by automobile, that is — and back again. As you know, the most of you, Mother got a year's leave from teaching at the Academy, and I, due to selling that strip of land by the lake to someone from away, plus certain other dealings, well, I come up with enough money to swing it, providin' we was prudent.

We had quite a list of acquaintances along the way, too — some of who we was able to warn ahead of time. We never stayed more than two-three days with any of them. They seemed cordial and glad to see us — for the most part. Of course we didn't *know* them all. Some were just cousins or such of folks we *did* know. But they was all some surprised to see us!

Well, nothing much happened going over New York State. I was kept pretty busy there counting my change at gas stations and diners, just to be sure. Not to mention them turnstiles they got on the free-ways. *Free-ways!* Godfrey! If we'd been smarter, we'da took the shunpikes.

I did take the wrong turn once, though. And hove up in this man's farm-yard. He seen the Vermont plates and figured I was from away. I asked him how to get back onto the main road and he says, "Well, mister, you just keep headed north and about seven miles up the road there's this big union school. Now, *four miles before* you get to that school, turn sharp left."

That man was a Smart Aleck, like so many of them people around New York State. We got back on the road, though, after some backing and filling, and was on our way again. The motor'd got het up some and so had Mother. The damned Smart Aleck — I mean that man, not Mother.

One night we bedded down with some friends of the Bert Higginses. You know Bert. That was somewheres in Ohio. They was some surprised to see us. They had a nice farm, but she wan't no hand at cooking. I can't say too little about it.

Well, sir, the next morning he (name was Henry something) went out to hitch up the horse to go into the village. Then he come in and et his breakfast and when he went out again that horse was lying on its side on the ground with the buggy half over, too. I heard Henry yelp and went out. Of course, I knew by just *looking*. That horse was *dead* — had died right there in the shafts. Well, old Henry poked it some with his toe and it was dead all right. And he says, "By Chrimus, that's a funny thing. This horse ain't never done *that* before."

I think it was somewheres in Ohio that I went into a store to buy Mother and me some cold tonic. It was hotter than Tophet that day and had been for quite a spell. Things looked all burned up and down at the mouth. And we was kinda dry ourselves. Well, sir, folks was having one hell of a argument in that store. Seems the town had to vote next day for or against putting in Daylight Saving Time. Finally, this one fellow bellowed out, "By golly, it's dry enough right now. I ain't going to vote for no damned Daylight Saving Time. Why, that extry hour of sunlight will *ruin* our crops."

We seen the Mississippi River the first time in Missouri. Had to, to get into Hannibal. Mother had caught sight of this old-time show boat tied up to the shore and wanted to go look at it. So later on we threshed around some and found it again. They'd made a sort of fancy diner out of it. And it was there I et my first catfish. Mother et veal. She's a might squeamish about catfish, having tried horned pout out of the pond back home. Well, catfish ain't nothing but a over-growed horned pout, anyways. I told Mother it was *good,* but a might gamier than horned pout. She said she wan't a bit surprised, considering what they pour into that river.

They had one fish there, stuffed and on the wall — the biggest fish I'd ever seen (took out of a stream, that is). I told the waiter that whoever caught that fish was a damned liar. Before we got off that boat they'd hooked us for almost two dollars and fifty cents.

After that we headed out over the state of Kansas. But I can't tell you much about the state of Kansas. It kept being the same all the time.

We had wanted to stay with this uncle of Eldon Baker's, near Hutchins, Kansas, but when we got there, folks was just coming home from *his* funeral, so we had to make other arrangements. We hadn't told them ahead of time we was coming, else they would of made better plans.

So Mother looked over the list and we went on to Garden City, Kansas, where Newton Freeley's wife's sister lives. We had wired them ahead but nobody was home when we got in the drive, so we had to stay in a motel called THE EASY REST. That was on a Monday. I remember I got to talking with the fellow who run the place. Now it so happened we'd had quite a long spell of very good weather and I said so, and he said, "Yes, damned good weather for a town this size."

When I paid the bill the next morning the proprietor said, "God, here it is Tuesday. Day after tomorrow'll be Thursday. My! How the week has flown."

After that we had quite a piece of wheeling. We no sooner got into Colorado than it commenced to spit snow. Not heavy, just spitting. But it was enough to slow me down some. I didn't know how they built their roads out there, being in a strange state. So we poked along awhile and come on this sign. "Road resurfacing," it read. "Go slow." I slowed up even more and went over the brow of the next little dip. And there was this great herd of cows being driven along on the road. Moving slow, too. Well, sir, them cows had done a pretty good job of resurfacing that road — from ditch to ditch, I'd say. What the snow hadn't done they'd took care of. Like I say, poor wheeling and a mighty skiddy road.

We ploughed around on that road for a spell, but finally drew up in the yard of these folks we *did* know, in Boulder, Colorado. We had phoned them ahead, long-distance, from Springfield, Illinoise. Cost us almost two dollars, but it was worth it. When we pulled in, there they was to greet us, right there on their front stoop. And was *they* a welcome sight!

It's awful sightly around their house in Boulder. The Rocky Mountains start right up from the far end of their plot of land.

Next morning I hosed the car off some. We seen *her* out in the garden putting in seed, so Mother and I went over to visit. Said she was putting in vegetables. I asked her what *kind* of seeds she was using.

"Burpee's," she said.

---

I says, "Oh, Burpee's — *Burpee's*! Well, them'll come up, all right."

Mother said, "Oh, *Francis.*" She had to smile though. But Lil didn't get it (her name was Lil).

That afternoon I give their little daughter one of the quart cans of maple syrup I had fetched along from Vermont. I opened it and dolloped out a little swallow for her. She took to it right away. About supper time she come into the house looking sort of peaked. She says, "Momma, I'm sick to my stomach." She wan't fooling, neither. She'd dropped the syrup can on the parlor rug and what was left in the can was coming out on the rug, too.

Next morning it seemed like the best policy for us was to head out West again. They told us which road to take. It went over something called the Berthoud Pass. "It'll be awful sightly," they told us.

Well, we started going *up* right away and it commenced to blow real hard and it snowed something wicked. Whenever it let up some and I looked off on one side, they was nothing over the bank but nothing — right straight down into *nothing*. Them folks hadn't told us a thing about no such wheeling as *that*! They both knew me and Mother gets giddy at heights.

Maybe I done wrong to give that little tyke of theirs *all* that maple syrup.

No wonder they call it a *Pass*! That's what I was doing all the ways over. What Mother done I don't know. But she lost some of her color, at least.

Well, we got down to the level again and commenced riding over Utah. We spent a night and most of a day in Salt Lake City where Mother done some laundry, mostly for me.

But speaking of *dry*. You ain't seen nothing till anybody gets onto that Salted Desert they got out there. Godfrey, no wonder them Mormons took on extry wives! They needed them, just to quench theirselves. (By fetching water, I mean.) Once I excused myself and stepped out of the automobile (since nothing was coming, either way). Well, sir, talk about *dry* ground! Not nothing to be seen but salt and then *more* salt!

It wan't long before we was into Nevada. Not too much happened there in spite of its reputation. We did stay for a short spell with my cousin Luman's folks near Elko. They was some surprised to see us, too.

Elko was where I seen my first *live* Indian. Talked to one of them, too. I started out by saying, "How . . ."

He says, "How *what*? Don't you speak English already?"

To get back to my cousin. Luman has this big cow farm there. He's a real card, too. Always joshing. Told me about this farmer had three acres of wooded land he wanted cleared so's he could put it to wheat. Luman says this farmer hired this fellow to do the job and the fellow came one morning with a single bitted axe to commence work.

The farmer said, "Just what do you expect to do with that axe? This is *three* acres of *trees* to be cleared off, not just a blackberry patch."

Well, the farmer went to town for the day and when he got back one whole acre was clean cut off. And he says, "By God, where'd you learn to do *that*? There ain't a tree left on that acre."

"I learned on the Sahara Desert," this fellow says.

"Why, you durned fool," the farmer says, "there ain't no *trees* on the Sahara Desert!"

And the fellow says, "Not any more, there ain't."

Well, we pulled out again and headed for California. We got a boy living out there which is why we was agoing anyways.

I hadn't counted on any more big mountains, but it

wan't long before we was up to the Sierras and I'm here to tell you *they* ain't no little mold hills. But we made it to the fur side, finally, and down into California. And I seen my first palm tree — which wan't in a tub, that is. They grow right out of the ground there. Our boy and his wife seemed glad to see us. They was some surprised, though. In no time they had gone out and fetched an extry bed from some folks they knew and asked us how long we expected to stay. They live in Berkeley, so we did, too. Had a nice long visit. She's a good cook, but a might too thin. Our boy had growed some, too — though sideways. They took us out to eat quite a bit, mostly to sea-food places. Crabs and other queer looking things. The boy said they was edible so I give them a try. They ain't too bad once you get them peeled. A little maple syrup might of helped some.

I suppose you'd like to know what grows in California. Mother took a fancy to all the growing things. As you know, she has a green thumb. All *I* can say about them growing things is *be careful.* There are some things out there I am awful kind of glad we don't have back here. Take that vine out near the boy's back stoop. Mother thought it was real sightly and fetched some indoors in a vase. But when the boy and his wife come home from work they let out this squawk. Claimed it was poison oak.

Well, two-three days later we decided to head back East. So two-three days later we headed back East. But we come home on the southern route. I says to myself, "No more of them mountain passes." Mother wouldn't of come home no other way anyhow. Said I carried on too much every time I got near one of them passes. Well, I do. Pinkham Notch is enough for me. As you all know, I was fetched up in a valley and I propose to be buried in one, spring freshets or no spring freshets.

I says to Mother, "Yes, sir, I propose to be buried in a

valley and I don't propose to fall into one on the way to my own funeral, neither.''

So we come home by the southern route. And seen a lot of sightly country doing it, too. One place, just into Texas, I dared Mother to go over to Mexico which we did. We stayed about an hour, looking around. It was the *first* foreign country I'd ever been in. I'm telling you, Mister, Mexico is one place you really need to button your wallet up tight. They all speak some foreign gibberish down there. I couldn't make out a thing they said, nor Mother neither, and she's a school teacher, too.

So we got back into Texas and headed east again. We kept heading east quite a few days before we seen the end of Texas. Talk about big! Godfrey, I imagine Orleans County would fit into it two-three times over.

We did stop to see Horace Beebe, though. You all remember his father, Grady. Minister in the Lower Village before he took his family away to Texas. Horace couldn't hardly believe his eyes when he seen us. His wife couldn't neither. They was some surprised.

Well, Horace had this big farm. He had a lot of cows he kept in this pasture of his'n to the right of his buildings. Horace called them ''white-faced cows.'' They had white faces is why, I presume.

One day while I was there I skipped into town for some tobacco and on the way back I picked up this little tyke. When we got near Horace's place I seen the cows all gone from the right-handed field, but they was a whole bunch in the left-handed field. And I says to this little boy, ''Them Horace's?''

He gave me a sort of a funny look and says, ''Horses? No, you durned fool, them's *cows*!''

We kept plugging along, going east, after we left Horace. To make a long story short, we commenced heading north and went accrost Louisiana and Georgia and Alabama and all them other southern states. I was a little edgy about our Vermont plates, but no one seemed to notice and we got through safe. But some of them roads they've got down there are a caution. I figure Henry Young could of went down there and showed them a thing or two about honing roads. Henry hones a pretty mean road when he's a mind to.

In Virginia we was going to stay with these in-laws of one of Mother's distant cousins. When we reached there about supper time they was having this gathering out on the lawn. They was some surprised to see us since they didn't ketch on *who* we was for a spell. Well, next day we headed north again and before anybody knew it we was into New York State and over the border into Vermont. We both commenced breathing easier right away.

Seton Falls was a mighty pretty sight to us, but when we got to the farm we seen we couldn't drive down our road, the mud was so deep. So we went to Luther Higbee's house for the night.

They was some surprised to see us.

## A Graduation Address

I have no idea why I am honored by this invitation to speak to you this evening, but I have a few suspicions. One of them is that I am one of the few native Vermont-born University of Vermont faculty left, you know; therefore, I am something of a curiosity, like the last surviving member of President Garfield's cabinet. Another of them is that I speak with a rather droll Vermont accent even when I don't intend to; therefore, again, I should be put on exhibition. Another is that I am the only one left who can be conned into getting up and making a public spectacle of himself. All of the rest of the boys now do it in print. Me, I am willing to do it publicly and let the chips fall where they may. And of course, finally, everybody knows that I have a dark suit. If you're going to speak in public, you have to have a dark suit.

As far as this particular bruhaha, or social, or strawberry festival and three-legged race, or annual meeting of the New England Pathological Marching and Chowder Society is concerned, I have been informed that my part of it should be on the lighter side and believe me, children, it's going to be. I've never been noted for my serious little inspirational messages. That kind of talk is always rather wretched. At least, it has always made me retch.

There's this rumor that has gotten around that I have a rather special love for an area in the State of Vermont known as the Northeast Kingdom. First of all, let me warn you about rumors. They are usually based on fact. And this particular one is most emphatically based on fact. Indeed, if my arm had not been bent — the one that reaches out for folding money —

I would undoubtedly be in the Northeast Kingdom right now, taking my ease in front of my Franklin stove, having first surrounded a martini — or two — or three.

But since I *am* here and since I have this *thing* about Vermont, we might as well talk about Vermont and then we can forget the whole damn thing and go home.

I have a feeling that some of you may be experiencing Vermont for the first time. So the least one can do for you is to try to explain a little bit about Vermonters and the odd state that they are in. But to explain Vermont to an outlander is, I am afraid, a little like trying to paint a picture not *of* jello but *with* it. Things don't come out quite the way you think they are going to. Or like blowing a saxaphone with your mouth full of alum. Not, God knows, that saxaphonists don't sound that way anyhow.

Now, to help you people from AWAY. And don't kid yourself about AWAY. To someone like me who comes from the Northeast Kingdom of Vermont, AWAY is a very real place. AWAY is somewhere south of Rutland, Vermont and nobody goes south of Rutland, Vermont — nobody goes downcountry — without first sewing his money inside his underwear. At least folks used to when they had underwear they could sew anything on to. Nowadays, of course, underwear is a little more scanty.

So, first, to help you people from AWAY who made the initial error of not having been born in Vermont, there are one or two stories that might help the situation. The first one has to do with a man from AWAY, from downcountry, probably from even as far away as Bennington. He came up to Orleans County during the fall bird shooting season and he ran out of ammunition, so he went into the general store in Craftsbury Common, Vermont where I have a summer place, and he said to the storekeeper, "Tell me, my good fellow, have you got any shot for grouse?" And the storekeeper said, "What did you say?" "Have you got any shot for grouse?" The storekeeper settled back on his heels and said, "Oh, for Chrissakes, you mean catridges for patridges?"

I spend a lot of time during my summer vacations sitting around in the Craftsbury store soaking up wisdom. That's where I was once watching the worst rainstorm in fifteen years come roaring down out of the sky and I heard Walter Wheeler turn around to me and say, "Well, Francis, it looks like rain, don't it?" And during the height of the 1938 hurricane I heard him say, "God, it's airy, ain't it?" I remember on one occasion, when a bolt of lightning had knocked out every light from Craftsbury Common to South Albany and back again by the southern route, he turned around and looked at me and said, "Well, Francis, there must be a frog in the wheel."

Walter is the one who lost a pig once and I heard that he'd lost it and I met him on the street — there's only one — and I said, "Walter, have you found your pig?" And he said, "Yes, by God, I've found my pig and when I found that pig, I'll tell you what I did to that pig. I kicked it, by gravy, all the way from Sheba to Bedam and back again." Well, obviously none of you have read your Bible, or you would enjoy that story a little bit more.

I'm sure Walter was the original of that famous — and I'm sure you all know this story — tale about the summer visitor who asked the native on the store step, "Have you lived here all your life?" and the native said, "No, not yet."

Well, all right, we have to get down to the business at hand. Now I suspect not too many of you have ever had the particular delight — benefit, let us say — of a graduation — commencement — address as given many years ago in the small high schools or academies of the Northeast Kingdom of Vermont, this fabled area.

Now, on these hot June occasions of many years ago, the speaker is usually a long-since retired member of the state legislature, or possibly the school superintendent of the next district to the north, or a relative of the local principal, the idea being, in that case, if there's any money involved by way of honorarium, let's, for God's sakes, keep it in the family. And recently, of course, there's been an alarming increase in appearances by University of Vermont faculty members. That is why I emphasize that this is a recollection of many years ago, because, of course, on this salary, I cannot afford to be sued.

These fine old cliches, these lovely old cliches bring tears to my eyes and I certainly hope you are going to water up some, too. This is a vanishing America that we want to preserve together for a moment this evening. It goes something like this and it's very hot. The speaker has come with his Come-to-Jesus collar on, but it has begun to wilt a little so he's had to loosen his tie. His suit was once black, but it has turned slightly green.

Well, it goes like this:

Superintendent Smith, Principal Brown, members of the school board, teachers, relatives, friends, but especially boys and girls. I am deeply honored to be asked on this happy but sad occasion to address the members of the graduating class of Goshen Academy. Let me first congratulate you on the originality of this motto which I see on the platform in back of me, handsewed, I am told, by the senior members of the home economics class: "Out of school life into life's school." What a thought! *What* a thought! It reminds me, members of this graduating class, of my own class motto of many, many years ago. In fact, it's the same motto.

Now, graduates, I hope you have thought on this word *commencement*. Does it mean the end of something? Why any booby knows better. What does *commencement* mean? It means, boys and girls, the *beginning,* the commencement — get it? — of that long road called *life.* A fine motto, indeed, you have chosen — "Out of the frying pan . . . Out of school life into life's school." And have you ever thought of life as a road? I have and I dare say one or two before me have. A road, frought with beware signs. For some of you a long road, for some, alas, short. For some smooth and level and easy and for some, up and down, and, if you'll excuse the expression, sort of rutty. And for some *c*ement, and by *c*ement I mean concrete. For others, wet and muddy, and by muddy, boys and girls, I mean terrible muddy.

Friends, I am reminded of a parable, the parable of the muddy road. Years ago during the deep mud season, my dear old father had to go from the farm to the village. Before I tell you that parable, let me tell you something about my dear old father. He taught at the State Agriculture College for thirty years and he was a revered member of the faculty there. His specialty was fertilizer. There are few graduates of the State Agriculture College who will forget his course called, "The Use and Abuse of Manure." My father was a dedicated teacher. I have had many of his graduates come up to me in later years, after he had been gathered to his fathers, and say, "I have never known a man so full of his subject."

But, boys and girls, to get back to the parable of the muddy road. That year the mud was so deep on the road that my poor old father had to use snowshoes on the road. As he approached the village he seen a hat lying on that muddy road which, as he came nearer, he observed to be moving. In some consternation, he picked up the hat to find the head of his friend and neighbor, Walter Wheeler.

"Walter," said my father, "you're in trouble, ain't you?"

"No," said Walter, "for I still have my horse under me."

Now, boys and girls, what can we learn from this parable? That it's best to keep something under us at all times? That it's best to stay to home where we belong? I'll tell you what we glean from this old anecdote — absolutely NOTHING.

As you travel along life's road, some of you will choose different *ruts*. Call them what you will, members of the graduating class, tire tracks, furrows, wheel marks, bicycle tracks, rabbit tracks, political trends — they are all ruts.

And what of these ruts? Why, boys and girls, they are the walks of life, the various callings. To each and every one of you (to coin a phrase) will come a call — your rut. Some of you will become lawyers, some doctors, some farmers, some lawyers, others doctors, and, of course, some of you won't. Some, alas, will just sit around or go bird hunting.

And that reminds me of the parable of the golden retriever. It seems Walter Wheeler bought himself a retriever — one of them duck-retrieving dogs — and he went out the first morning of his proud ownership and went duck hunting. He went into his duck *blind*. A herd of them ducks come over. Walter lifted his gun and he shot one of them ducks and the duck went into the water and that dog retrieved the duck, but how did he do it? Members of the graduating class, that dog walked along the top of the waters and retrieved that duck. Walter was somewhat took aback, but he said to himself, "I *was* in Hardwick last night. And I stayed kinda late. I stayed till almost ten o'clock. I better not decide about this thing until tomorrow."

So he waited until the next morning and he went out again shooting ducks and he shot a duck and the dog indeed retrieved the duck by walking along the top of the waters. By this time Walter was kinda scared, and he called his neighbor Foster Kinney up and said, "Foster, I got an awful odd acting dog. I'd like you should come duck hunting with me tomorrow morning and see if I'm wrong about this dog." And Foster said, "I will as soon as my chores are done," and he did. And the next morning they both went into that duck blind and they both shot a duck and that dog walked along the top of the waters and retrieved both of them ducks. And Walter looked at Foster and said, "I told you they was something wrong with that dog. Will you tell me what it is?" And Foster looked at Walter and said, "There's nothing wrong with your dog. It just can't swim."

Boys and girls, I mentioned doctors a while ago and that puts me in mind of another parable, the parable of the young wolf in the doctor's office. It seems a young wolf, feeling poorly, visited a doctor's office. There in the waiting room he found his friend the fox.

"Well, wolf," says fox, "you poorly?"

"Yes," says wolf.

"Well sir," says fox, "this doctor is a real hum-dinger, a real wing-ding. You see that elk just leaving? Well, he had ptomaine pizen and the doc cut off his toe."

"That so?" says wolf, getting kinda edgy.

"Yes sir," says fox, "and see that rabbit just leaving? Well, he had erysipelas and the doc cut off his ears."

"That so?" says wolf, kind of thoughtful. And by now he was looking sorta peaked. And he grabbed his hat and left, saying, "I'm going to grab my hat and leave. I've got *asthma.*"

Now then, some of you *will* be doctors, or lawyers,

or teachers (God forbid!) and some farmers, which last, by a most fortuitous train of thought, leads us to the old parable of the thrifty farmer.

It seems there was a thrifty farmer who hitched his wagon to a — horse — and each Saturday went to the Hardwick Trust Company to deposit the milk check and whatever other modest sums he had received from fleecing — from helping the summer folk. This went on for some years.

Now, boys and girls, one Saturday this farmer came to the Hardwick Trust Company at 11:55 A.M., just before closing time, and asked to *take out* $200.00. Well sir, as the line of customers grew longer and longer behind him, the farmer's $200.00 was counted out in $20.00 bills.

"Mr. Teller," says the farmer, "I kinda wanted that in smaller denominations."

So, as the line grew even longer and closing time had already arrived, the teller laboriously counted out the $200.00 in fives and ones.

At last he said, "There!"

"Just a minute," says the farmer, "I believe I'll count it myself, just to be sure."

"Fudge," says the teller. But slowly the farmer counted out his money, from front to back and then from back to front.

"Well, you old coot," says the teller, "it's all there, ain't it?"

"Yes," says the farmer, "it's all there — just *barely.*"

Let me tell you, too, as you are leaving these hollow halls so overgrowed with ivory, the hoary myth of the young man with six hundred gold pieces.

It seems a young man inherited six hundred gold pieces from a maiden aunt from up Beebe way by the name of Letty. Now, being a young man and therefore sort of twitchy, he took off for that modern Sodom, Burlington, Vermont. In two weeks he was back home (as so often happens in these parables), stoney broke and somewhat hung over. And he took a reckoning. And he said, "Where did Aunt Letty's six hundred gold pieces go? I spent two hundred of them gold pieces on alcoholic beverages, including tax. And another of them two hundred gold pieces I spent on sightly women which was somewhat taxing, too. But the final two hundred, the last two hundred of them gold pieces? Where did they go? *Them* I must of squandered."

Well, I can tell you this about that young man (and this line has to be in every graduation address or it ain't official), that young man had more wishbone than backbone. Otherwise he'd have spent more on the sightly women.

Ah yes, lawyers, doctors, nurses — *nurses*! Another parable comes to mind gleaned from a brief teaching sojourn up toward Beebe Junction, but, alas, that parable must remain untold. That nurse is still alive. And so am I in a sort of counterfeit way.

However, the parable of the counterfeiters comes to mind — the New York State counterfeiters who had very successfully been making ten and twenty dollar bills for some years and decided they was a mite bored with it, so they turned out a number of eighteen dollar bills. After they had made quite a pile of them, they decided it would be best to unload them, and they didn't know where to unload them, but decided on Eden Mills, Vermont. They went up there by car and the leader of the counterfeiters went into the store with one of them eighteen dollar bills and said to the storekeeper, "Tell me, my good fellow, have you got any of them smoking cigarettes?" And the storekeeper said, "I believe I do." The counterfeiter said, "Could you change an eighteen dollar bill?" And the storekeeper said, "I believe I can. Would you like three sixes or two nines?"

Now, boys and girls, a number of things have been left unsaid and they can't be because they always *are* said at graduation exercises. We must not slight them today.

First, there is the "as you look back motif."

Graduates, as you look back through dimming eyes to these happy days at Goshen Academy; when you remember your carefree, happy, even slap-happy fellow scholars; the corn huskings; the apple parings; the sleigh rides you was taken for; when you look at the quilting parties — then the tears will fill your eyes, the lumps will lump in your throats and you will say, holding your self-chosen (but God-given) life mate by the hand, "Lottie, ain't you glad we don't have to live through none of *that* crud again!"

Second, there is the "hold the torch high" motif.

Boys and girls, the torch is yours. We old ones give it to you with faltering hands. We didn't always carry it high and clear. We throw it to you. Catch it. Hold it high. Watch out for the drippings.

Third, there is the "it is better to have" motif.

Now, when I was a member of the state legislature in 1907, I used to ride my English bicycle to Montpelier every week. As you know, an English bicycle has no foot brake. You can peedle it backwards while you coast forwards. I used to coast through Northfield, Vermont peedling backwards. It give them folks quite a start.

And there's a moral to this part of the story. Don't believe all you see going on in Northfield, Vermont.

Now, graduates, there's a trick to riding a bicycle all day long without getting tired. Jack your seat up high enough so that you flex your legs every time you peedle. I might say, though, that no matter how high you get your seat up and no matter how much you flex your legs, you can't ride a bicycle all day without one thing getting tired, real tired, and I'll tell you what that is, members of this class — your shoulders.

Well, sir, I was joshed some about that bicycle when I used to come wheeling up to the legislature. They called me Scorcher Colburn. One day one of my opponents — I believe he was a member of the Bull Moose party — said to me on the floor of the House that I seemed to be peedling backwards most of the time. Friends, I answered that man. I got up and looked him square in the eye and, using the immortal words of the immortal Bard from the immortal Avon, I said to him, "It is better to have done it backwards than never to have done it at all."

Friends, that man was silenced leave alone confused.

Fourth, the "let me give you some practical advice" motif which is always included in graduation exercises. My aged Aunt Hattie had a fine old Vermont recipe handed down from generation to generation. It goes like this: TAKE A QUARTER OF A POUND OF CHEESE. That's all. My Aunt Hattie used to say it was not only a recipe but, if circumstances warranted, a kind of a cure, too.

Boys and girls, that recipe is a good deal like the practical advice I'd like to leave with you today. On this thorny journey, no matter what the odds, through thick or thin, fat or lean, Democrat or Republican, death or taxes, sulphur or molasses — *whatever* the circumstances — DON'T.

There has never been a graduation address without a little bit of inspirational verse. Since I was not able to find any inspirational verse, I made my own and here it is. It's called, "To Goshen's Sons and Daughters":

Here's to Goshen's sons and daughters,
Leaving the harbor for deeper waters.

As you quit these shallow shoals
Your vision fix on highest goals.

Be tempered by this guiding thought:
Don't do things you hadn't ought.

If your path gets deep and muddy
And the going's kind of cruddy,

Hark to these, my warning words:
Life's more likely whey than curds.

Like a beagle scenting rabbits,
Point your nose toward cleanly habits.

Some make saints and some make sinners,
Big fish grow from little minners.

Whilst you're ploughing through the breakers,
Don't be slackers, don't be fakers.

Whilst you're faring on life's ocean,
Think of Mother, think of Goshen.

Peedling with your rear end high,
Yours is not to reason why.

And if life's a bitter cup,
Don't turn aside and throw it up.

Finally, boys and girls, I'd like to leave you with this thought. As I look into your bright and shining faces this day, I can only say this, "GOD HELP THE STATE OF VERMONT!"

# III.  A Teacher, God Forbid

# Talk Before a Teachers' Convention

I am not too sure of my function here today since I am not a public school teacher, nor do I have much to do, save indirectly, with preparing teachers for their careers. Most of my students at the University of Vermont hope to be doctors, lawyers, farmers or lieutenant governors, and (in great numbers and with very special hope) wives.

According to the program, we are examining the needs and faults and virtues of a currently popular character named Johnny whose reading ability has come recently under considerable fire and whose teachers have been dodging bombs like those unfortunates who had to dodge the egg when it hit the electric fan.

To put it in the vernacular of our beloved Northeast Kingdom, "Johnny don't read good."

My own part in these heady festivities has to do with Johnny's relation to art. He is, of course, a much younger person than those with whom I must contend at the University. However, I do have recollections of Johnny, going back an alarming number of years, and even some notions about his art life.

What we can discuss here exists on a number of levels. Since our time is limited, it seems wise to direct our investigation to the more obvious levels. And, if you will forgive me, I would prefer not to attempt a little inspirational talk, but to say fairly plainly what I seem to see from this possibly clouded corner.

What we do with Johnny in art class depends on our reasons for getting him into it in the first place. If we want to make an artist of him, we are sunk. Democracy in education has many virtues, I am sure (although why some folks aspire to a college degree remains a dark and soul-searing enigma). The realistic fact is that no amount of democratizing is going to make Johnny an artist if he isn't one, any more than endless and expensive music lessons will make a good farm hand into another Paganini or Satchmo Armstrong. I doubt if any harm has ever been done in exposing even the most loutish of young oafs to the creative process unless he gets illusions of artistic grandeur. Teachers College of Columbia University did education no favor when it suggested that every single one of the little darlings is a potential artist. In ninety-nine cases out of one hundred, the best we can hope for (and it's a really admirable best at that) is a better and more charitable comprehension of the nature of art, a lessening of this damnable and frightening current tendency toward conformity, a fresher eye with which to see and enjoy the efforts of real artists, and a modest freeing up of the imagination. These are the possibilities public school art can offer most Johnnys and Janies. And certainly good is done if a student here and there picks up an engrossing hobby to alleviate those bleak times in later life when the cake falls, the biscuits burn, or Johnny himself comes too late from the Fair — the Barton Fair, of course.

If such do-it-yourself (and I mean really do-it-*yourself*) ventures are pursued, it might at the least lessen the popularity of one of the greatest immoralities of our century — the numbered painting, in which the artistic sustenance has been thoroughly pre-chewed and partially pre-swallowed. (And we won't follow *that* little figurative flight to its logical conclusion.)

Possibly the most important reward I have named is the freeing of the imagination. It may, as I have said, be a modest freeing, but it is good for even the sow's ears and has far-reaching implications for that rare student who turns out to be a real purse in matters of art.

Your responsibilities here are almost frightening. In so brief a time, I can say only this: (you fill in the rest).

The fewer cut out pumpkins and patterned Santa Clauses and stenciled tulips the better. And the more paper, brushes, poster paint and being left alone the better too.

The process of art is one of self-discovery. It is also one of invention. No child has ever come within light years of either self-discovery or invention when confronted with a stenciled tulip precisely like his neighbor's and a red crayon also monotonously like his neighbor's.

There is a right way to spell *alleviate.* And learning to spell *alleviate* involves certain painful rote processes (to which I was apparently not subjected because I had to look it up when I wrote this sentence). But the process of art is *not* rote. It is personal, private, and the ground rules are few. Stencils have nothing to do with it.

In the freedom to explore which must be granted children as they pursue art, remember that the symbols and visions of childhood are not those of adults. Don't force Johnny's proudly conceived mess into *your* version of a tree until he asks you to. And even then, don't pull it too far away from *his* version. He may know, intuitively, more about art than you ever will. He may know, for example, that art and nature are two very different things, and that nature is *not* art's ultimate goal, but its point of departure.

Until Vermont school systems are willing to sacrifice in some area to make room for good trained art supervisors, I don't think much more can be said in this direction.

The other level we might touch upon involves Johnny's

surroundings, including the pictures on his classroom walls. I hope things have changed since I was Johnny. It is a fact that I had no idea a picture involved anything except noxious tones of sepia brown until advanced childhood. The brown reproduction of Botticelli's "Birth of Venus" over the piano at home didn't help any, either. Get those grim reproductions of "The Pilgrim's Going to Church" off the wall. (Why, oh why didn't someone paint Thomas Morton and the Indian maidens dancing around the maypole at Merry Mount? No one would necessarily *have* to tell the children that everyone at Merry Mount had had quite a go at the rum jug.) Put up, instead, color reproductions of Degas' ballet dancers, and Cezanne's still-lifes, and Van Gogh's exciting landscapes. Even Picasso's blue guitar player, and his wonderful early paintings of children.

Biased as I am, I *know* — not just modestly suggest — that a school system has as much obligation to buy such pictures for its children as it has to buy them soft-ball bats.

On this level something about art can be imparted to children by verbalizing about the pictures, but even more by the simple alchemy of the blotting pad. A child who has lived a part of every day for a month with Van Gogh's "Cypress Trees" is going to realize, sooner or later, that it is a better picture than Mr. Leutze's "Washington Crossing the Delaware," or a brown reproduction of Henry Wadsworth Longfellow's hairy face, or an over-blown and highly improbable colored photograph of a Vermont covered bridge. The wondrously intense imagination evident in Van Gogh's painting might set Johnny's imagination off. It won't make him an artist. And why should it? Most artists get that way in spite of rather than because. If they don't, they are probably plumbers at heart anyway.

Johnny may very well become a plumber, or a doctor,

or a farmer, or a schoolteacher. But plumbers and doctors and farmers and lieutenant governors and, dear God, how emphatically, schoolteachers are no good without a great deal of imagination. And a nodding acquaintance with *good* art, which *is* imagination, makes for *better* plumbers and farmers and teachers and housewives.

1960

## Sows' Ears and Purses

Archibald MacLeish, speaking of his poetry writing class at Harvard, once said, ". . . if they come in sows' ears they are going out sows' ears." The implication is that only God and a proper adjustment of genes will produce a poet (and, by extention, a painter, sculptor, composer, dancer or actor).

I'm afraid MacLeish was right. A teaching career which began shortly after the Second Battle of Bull Run and shows every sign of going on forever (a student recently guessed my age at thirty-eight!) has convinced me of his wisdom.

In the heady days of young manhood, when first I joined this faculty as that odd fish-bowl inhabitant called "resident artist," I would have looked upon MacLeish's remark as the bitter croak of a tired old frog. In that long-gone time I even told a Dean of Women that I could teach her how to paint. Bless her for not putting me to the test.

We might as well face the fact that while artists come about largely by accident, some sort of *thing* has to be there in the first place. The accident which sets off the process of creating is astonishing in its variety. If the accident never happens to the individual to whom it *should* happen, that unhappily passed-over individual has, to the end of his days, an itch which he can't scratch. The new tranquilizing drugs are useless.

One of the reasons for art courses in college is setting the stage for an accident, just in case. If the rare individual with the unaccountable itch discovers that when he is painting or sculpting, acting or playing a fiddle he knows exactly where to scratch, we probably have an artist on our hands.

But this rare individual is indeed rare. No art teacher

with his marbles intact expects to produce many artists. No English teacher expects to produce many writers, after the first few missionary years. As a matter of fact it is somewhat frightening to recognize, and in some way bear responsibility for, the exceptional purse amongst the hundreds of amiably flapping sows' ears. It's a little like playing toss and catch, bare-handed, with a tennis ball and having the ball arrive in your hands, on one throw, an extremely hot potato.

So in Heaven's name why teach art? Most art teachers (all of ours, by the way) are pretty excited about the undertaking because they really believe the old saw about man's not living by bread alone. They are sure that art is one of man's crowning glories, quite as worthy as the discovery and use of antibiotics or the achievement of the hydrogen bomb. (Or isn't that the latest and most effective one?) They want to pass the good word along because they are convinced that potentially good engineers and doctors and diplomats and inventors of super-effective bombs will be better ones if somewhere along the line, preferably early, they are exposed to the humanizing influence of the arts.

Allowing for understandable biases, they are not overly concerned with whether the exposure comes through studio courses in painting, sculpture or crafts, art history courses, a drama or dance workshop, or in indoctrination into the structure and sound of a Mozart quartet. It surely can come about through wisely guided efforts in creative writing.

One of *my* biases is toward the studio arts. Studio courses have virtue even for the vast majority not afflicted with the true call. Such courses offer — indeed demand — the creative act. And the veriest dolt becomes a better dolt when he discovers the rewards of the creative act. Studio courses by their nature needle the imagination into functioning. A well-oiled imagination is a blessing in any profession, including that of housewife. (If our national imagination had once been better exercised, that great American immorality, the paint-by-number kit, could never have gained its shameful foothold.)

History of art courses always point up man's never ending attempt to give shape and meaning to his environment and his life. We hope history of art students will be tempted to join the struggle as they shape their own environments.

I suspect MacLeish, had he been cornered, would have admitted that the students attending his poetry writing workshop came out of the experience wiser and more delighted readers of poetry, even if not producers of it.

Art teachers hope their charges will emerge with an understanding of the difference in purpose between a *Saturday Evening Post* cover and Picasso's Guernica mural. I suspect that good music teachers hope their students will approach, genuflect before and pass *through* Tschaikowsky, and on to Mozart, Bach and even Carl Orff. Surely good English teachers know that Thomas Wolfe has to be tasted in one's youth, but hope to proselyte in the direction of a more mature taste.

No university should let its product loose upon the world without having had a good hard brush with one or more of the arts. The institution whose graduate once asked Toscanini, "Tell me, sir, just what *are* Brahms?" is to be condemned. The other, whose graduate student announced a dislike for Kipling "because it has so many bones in it" should also hang its head. Very true, we can't expect a purse every time. But some sows' ears are handsomer than others.

Malcolm Cowley once expounded to me the theory of the three convolutions. On the first convolution one is enamored of Strauss waltzes, cover illustrations by Norman Rockwell, mystery novels by Agatha Christie and sometimes (God forbid) verse by Edgar Guest.

On the second convolution one spurns these seemingly too popular expressions and turns one's allegiance *exclusively* to Bach and/or Orff, to Paul Klee, to Franz Kafka. (This is the stage at which one often takes up the playing of the recorder, in exclusive little groups.)

But on the third convolution a mellow wisdom sets in. One loves the glories of Bach and *also* the winy charm of Strauss. One laughs or weeps unabashed at the truth of Rockwell's cover illustrations and comprehends as well the wonder of Paul Klee's work. One reads Agatha Christie because it's fun and *also* Kafka (which is not always fun).

The point is that one has learned not to be a snob, but rather a wise gourmet whose sensibilities appreciate things for what they aim to be. A fried egg is not the same as *galantine de veau en gelee.* Both are edifying to the hungry man, depending on his gastronomic mood. In the arts only the limited mind can afford to be snobbish. Conceivably another function of college art courses is to help older young fry reach the admirable third convolution.

Not long ago many scientists prided themselves on their lack of patience with the "frivolity" of the arts and most emphatically condemned them in college curricula. But also not long ago the Massachusetts Institute of Technology, that great brooder-house for scientists, saw its lack of vision in not offering its students experience in the arts and, forthwith, established courses to remedy the situation.

Let us hope we are well away from the extreme theory once expounded by teachers' colleges that every blessed little second-grader is a potential artist and will actually be one, given the proper freedom to express himself. Well, he isn't. Most second-graders don't and never will itch in the right place. As we all know, only a kind fate has prevented some of them from having two heads. But the fact still remains that they should *all* be given a chance to find out about themselves and their possible relation to the arts.

A good doctor who is also a good 'cellist is doubly worthy and doubly content. Einstein played a good second violin. It is an odd fact that recently evening classes in painting, sculpture and crafts have been besieged by scientists, who comment wistfully that they wish they had done it long ago. It is interesting that nowadays one can go to any medical center in the country (including ours) and find amongst the younger resident doctors the makings of an enthusiastic string quartet.

To be sure, not all insurance men are poets of the stature of insurance man Wallace Stevens. But insurance men and lawyers, doctors and storekeepers, lumbermen and bakers all have become avid and wise buyers of art, not for speculation but for private enjoyment.

Something is afoot. Curiosity about the arts is rampant in America, but it is something more than curiosity. It is also something more than vogue. Surely it is something more than easy money and leisure. Could it be, in an explosive and frightening world, a reaching out for something with which to bolster the spirit? Could it be a recognition that America's Madison Avenue version of success has some specious aspects, that something pretty damned important has been left out?

Maybe college art courses will increasingly guide the reaching out, help identify the overlooked ingredient. We know the sows' ears will always vastly outnumber the purses. This is true in professional art schools and music conservatories. No training yet conceived by man will make the basically inept anything but more complicatedly inept. Those who are only romantically or frivolously interested in proving themselves artistic purses never worry art teachers, or music or creative writing teachers. In time such misguided souls become resounding croppers. If the teachers are charitable, this happens early in the attempt.

The real purses are what they are. The genes are right and (if you want to look at it that way) God has smiled upon them. God speed them. But the hundreds of others? They are the ones doing the groping, having the curiosity, searching for the missing ingredient. They usually have the wit to know that no course in college or anywhere else will magically make them artists. They are also wise in knowing that art courses have other aims and compensations. And they are not really sows' ears at all. I just said that.

1960

# Art and Change

Let us assume you have had trouble, too, with modern art. Let us be reassured, however, that others have tried to admire, or at least understand, modern painting — an abstraction, for example — and have had no small difficulty even in the simple matter of holding it right side up. This alone can have a chilling effect, but then there is the further difficulty of the odd shapes with which to contend. Somehow these shapes have to be interpreted. After all, any picture has to *mean* something. Pray, what *do* these shapes represent?

The key to the whole knotty problem may lie in that word *represent*. It is quite possible that these odd shapes, and thus the whole picture, do not represent anything at all! They may simply constitute a design important only for its own sake. But this sounds glib. We'd better dig a little deeper.

The history of art is a series of revolutions and counter-revolutions. A way of painting becomes established (not without pain, as you will see) and the individual artists who adhere to this established and publicly favored mode of laying pigment on canvas gradually acquire standing — even respect — in their community. Things seem rather pleasant all around, with very little name-calling, and the individual artist may grow a beard as a mark of dignified social responsibility, much as a young bank clerk, promoted to second assistant treasurer, takes up cigars.

Then certain young upstarts with probably dangerous, and certainly zany, notions of what constitutes art appear on the artistic horizon. They clamor and hoot with derision at the established artists, call them greybeards, and issue manifestoes proclaiming themselves the *avant garde* of the new artistic enlightenment. It always comes as a shock to these brave young painters (and writers and composers) when other and even younger ones appear to point out that the brave young painters are now actually in their sixties, are being relieved of responsibility for art's future, and that the *avant garde* of an even newer age of artistic enlightenment is mercifully taking over.

Of course this is serious over-simplification of the story. The time-lag varies and the circumstance doesn't always work out in quite this way, but our simplification may serve to explain one of the first things we must comprehend if we are to make sense of modern, or any other, art: Historically *art is never static.*

Since time began man's artistic expressions and communications have been constantly changing. This is not to say that they have been improving. It simply means that as artists have emerged, in different times, countries, economic and political milieus, and with varying degrees of emotional upheaval or quietude, they have found at hand different means with which to achieve artistic utterance and, indeed, different subjects upon which to make utterance.

The obvious result is that a painting produced in the culture of fifteenth-century Flanders is not like one generated from the culture of twentieth-century America. And it is unwise to compare such pictures on the basis of greater or lesser merit. It is more profitable to note *how* they differ. Thus one may come to realize that each is of merit in relation to its time and place and not necessarily measurable by the same yardstick. Some peoples in some ages develop a high regard for their own art, as did the Italians of the Renaissance. In other times other peoples are slow to understand the authenticity of their own artistic expression.

Go to the library and ask for a book of color reproductions of paintings by the Impressionists. Find particularly the landscapes. Rather mild stuff? Nothing controversial in these pleasant and sun-drenched scenes? Certainly not; in fact, they are quite reminiscent of the most conservative landscapes of our own age. But less than a century ago all of France was up in arms against the monsters who painted them. There was no detail! The paint was put on in great, crude gobs of pure color! One had to stand fifteen feet away to make any sense at all out of these sloppily executed horrors! It was years before the Impressionists, whose work seems to us so gentle, so understandable and lovely, were taken seriously.

Now we begin to have something to go on. We can see that art changes as times change. Artists think and act upon different premises in different ages and places, and we can agree that the art of now has a right to look different from the art of another era. We can be assured also (if history continues its pattern) that the art of the future will be different from that of now, and legitimately so, since the time and place will be a new time and place.

Let us consider another aspect of the problem. Some art is objective and some is subjective. Most of us have seen more of the objective than of the subjective, and are still trying to understand the latter with means better suited to understanding the former. A typically objective picture — a story-telling *Saturday Evening Post* cover, for example — offers no problem in understanding. It's all there, told for us down to the last detail, in familiar form and comfortable technique. There is no doubt about which way up it should be held. And we enjoy it immensely for its clever, if transient, story-telling merits, as indeed we should, unless we are the silliest sort of artistic snob.

Typically subjective pictures — among them many of the

works of modern artists — present, on the other hand, considerable difficulty unless we bring to them a somewhat different kind of appreciative equipment from that employed in looking at the magazine cover. In the first place a subjective piece may not have a story-telling purpose. It may well be conceived as an arrangement of shapes, colors and textures that germinated within the painter's mind rather than from a visible model. It may be a highly intellectual and calculated exploration of geometry. Again, it may be an attempt to put down on canvas the painter's sensation of fear, destruction, or peace. In yet another instance there may be elements of realism involved — vaguely recognizable fruits, guitars and napkins on an almost table. This means that the artist has re-organized his visible, tangible models into a different kind of order from that in which they actually rest, and one more pleasing to him. In each case it becomes apparent that modern art has a greater or lesser degree of subjectivity, depending upon the degree of liberty taken by the artist with his material.

Again it looks as if we have something to go on. It would appear that there are roughly two ways of pursuing the making of a picture. One is based on the concept that art is, in a very real sense, a mirror up to nature, and that the more exactly *like* its subject a picture is, the greater its merit. This point of view demands from the painter a great technical facility in copying, an ability to match colors well, considerable patience, the reining in of the imagination, and a certain lack of curiosity. It frequently results in somewhat trite recordings of the literal appearance of covered bridges, birch trees, and snow scenes.

The second is based on an entirely different idea of the purpose and practice of art. Its major premise is that art is a creative process, not the undertaking of careful copying, and that artists are inventors and creators, not copyists. Adherents of this view insist that, whereas such technical equipment as sound drawing ability and knowledge of the application of paint are presupposed, these are only the painter's tools, not ends in themselves. His most important tool they consider his imagination. No amount of technical skill alone, they say, can produce art; such skill has value only as handmaiden to the creative and inventive impulse. This concept of art produces often challenging and on occasion extremely obscure work.

In the case of modern art, invention appears to us the most dominant characteristic. Inventing means making something new. We must become familiar with new things before we can experience them fully. Remember your first ripe olive?

So here we are, with everything tidily separated and labeled "copying" or "inventing," "objective" or "subjective." Alas, how superficial all this tidiness! Because of course the fact is that the categories get completely mixed up, the pigeon-holes often dissolve into one confusing catch-all, and there is really neither "typical" traditionalism nor "typical" modernism; that a lot of primitive African, or sophisticated Egyptian, or decorative Persian art looks very modern indeed; that many of the figures in the paintings of the twentieth-century Mexican Orozco are astonishingly like those of the thirteenth-century Italian Giotto. And that some contemporaries of the modern school use realistic effects, while some contemporaries of the conservative school use abstract devices.

All is not lost, however. We have merely arrived at the sensible realization that there are degrees in all things. Let us consider three artists, each of whom makes a picture from the same fruit, cloth and pitcher arranged on a table. The first artist paints carefully and lovingly an exact representation of the subject as it appears, delineating each with verisimilitude.

He produces a convincingly life-like facsimile and is very happy. The second artist feels that a rearrangement of the fruit, cloth and pitcher would make a more interesting design and possibly heighten the significance of his picture in terms of space relationships. This rearranging he effects by reshuffling the objects, not on the table but *on his canvas*. When he applies color he decides that, whereas the fruit is actually red, it will better serve the purposes of his particular design to paint it blue. This he does, and then adds a bit of blue to the wall where actually there is none. His final product is a personal comment, in paint, on the subject of fruit, cloth and pitcher — a painting *about* the subject, not *of* it — and he also is happy.

The third painter, who is probably sharing the studio because of a momentary financial embarrassment so familiar to artists, has a third point of view about it all. He takes a considered look at the fruit, cloth and pitcher, turns his back on them and produces an abstraction whose great charm lies in its inventiveness. In this case the material serves only as the point of departure for a creative design whose meaning is inherent in the shapes he arranges and the colors he chooses. His work will have more or less meaning according to how much or how little the observer can see. In any case this last picture will not be a substitute for the real fruit, cloth and pitcher, but rather a self-sufficient entity, important, if at all, for its own sake. By imbuing his design with such colors as deep blues, greens and even black, the third artist might direct our emotions into paths of quiet or foreboding, or he might employ reds, yellows and lighter blues and greens to give us a sense of quickened vitality — even joy.

If all three painters achieve their goals, then all three are legitimately happy. Which one is *right*? Which one is *best*? There was once in one of my classes a delightful elderly gentleman who took up painting late in life, as a hobby. He had spent years teaching mathematics. His consuming interest became the production of Vermont landscapes, but he found a number of stubborn little problems in his way. One day he presented me, with some anxiety, a book of landscape paintings in reproduction, pointing out, as he thumbed the pages, that here an artist had made the light on his mountains come from the left and here another had cast the light from the right. "In God's name," he said, "which is correct?"

If you can understand why our second painter felt impelled to rearrange and distort, and take liberties with color, then it will eventually become easier for you to understand our third painter's *total* devotion to invention.

You will, for example, accept as reasonable the proposition that part of the meaning of modern art lies in its mystery; that painters can't explain their work in words (else they would have written rather than painted) and that pictures are to be looked at, not read, as music is to be heard. You will be quite unperturbed at the fact that art does not lend itself to the kind of analysis demanded by those who so tirelessly and tiresomely insist on word-meaning. Remembering that all art is related to, and has special if occasionally belated significance for, its own age, it will occur to you that some contemporary painters find within themselves the uncertainty and turmoil of their times, and that they reflect these conditions quite literally on their canvases. Your traditional sensibilities may at times be offended, but you will not lose sight of the fact that art is inclusive, with bases resting upon all of life, not just upon its most pleasant aspects. Our times offer peculiar and unfamiliar juxtapositions, strange distortions, broken patterns. Quite logically some of our art does, too.

Don't for a moment think that an increasing understanding of modern art precludes a love of traditional art. The mark of an artistically literate person is the breadth of mind which allows for delight in *all* art, and which makes unnecessary the fruitless pitting of one aspect of art against another.

There is good reason for curiosity about these things. Education, we are rightly and repeatedly told, must go beyond the technical training of adequate engineers, chemists, teachers and doctors. It must in some way help students to become happier people, so that they can become *very good* engineers, chemists, and so on. Intimate knowledge of the various arts contributes immeasurably to the fulfillment of the individual, whatever his profession.

1952

# For the Time Being

"Silent" generations are nothing new. There have been numerous ones throughout recorded history and the results of their existence, and silence, have not been calamitous. This particular generation of silent ones has had a great deal to digest and whatever public silence it affects is probably commendable.

We are at a disadvantage in having to compare those who, we feel, should be currently sounding the alarms of a new age with immediately preceding generations of astonishing articulateness. Possibly we have been deluded by recent loud noises on almost all fronts of human endeavor, but most especially on those of the creative arts, into thinking that *most* generations are astonishingly articulate. Of course this is not so. Nor does it follow that what seems, at the moment, silence in the now emerging generation connotes stupidity, torpor or fright. There is, as already suggested, an unusual amount to digest.

By now it is redundant to point out that extraordinary changes in values, on all levels, are part of this generation's inheritance. New concepts of meaning have undermined comfortable old standards of "good" and "bad." With the merest flick of the diplomatic eyebrow a time-honored international policy is exactly reversed. Official friends become official enemies. Distance diminishes and with it, somehow, time.

Thought control is a recognized and officially admired technique. "Peace" is not everywhere an entirely acceptable word. As for the atom bomb . . . And so it goes, wherever you care to look. All of these issues have two sides and traditionally one should be less moral than the other. Morality, alas, seems to change with geography and with the flick of that diplomatic eyebrow.

Or with one's artistic taste. A large body of otherwise unhysterical citizens know — not merely suspect — that modern art is communistic. Read recent commentary on this year's sculpture show at the Metropolitan Museum. But Communist Russia knows with equal certainty that modern art is degenerate and bourgeois and will have none of it.

Yes, there is a lot to digest.

It has always been the privilege of youth to be cock-sure and noisily so. Apparently the present crop chooses to do a little evaluating before it sounds off. Despite lack of public utterance, there are intimations that the evaluating goes on. Throughout the country there are young novelists and poets and composers and painters hard at work on important things. To deny this is sheer nonsense and denotes a very shallow examination indeed.

My concern is with the painters.

Universities are rarely seedbeds of new expression in art. Indeed, few practicing artists ever go to college since few colleges have room in their curriculum for the training required, preferring as they do to examine what has already been done rather than to sponsor the actual doing.

It is then to art schools of professional standard we must turn to discover the intimations of evaluation. And in them is a noticeable ferment. One cannot imagine such tumult long being contained within the art schools alone. In their own time the artists of the "silent" generation will take over the gallery walls and "silent" will become, for them at least, a wildly inappropriate label.

The story is long and complicated and, like all of the story of art, involves a series of revolutions, counter-revolutions, periods of surface peace and sudden eruption, often accompanied by great bitterness. The present periods of peace and eruption are developing faster than we are accustomed to, and the layman — the already confused and suspicious public — is two or three phases back of current events. The layman is, indeed, still making up his mind about the virtues of modern art versus those of academic (realistic) art, while the events of significance to this age, the revolts and counter-actions, are all taking place within the rather loose framework of modern art.

Specifically (and, I fear, in over-simplified version), this is what is going on: there exists a school of non-objective art, whose adherents' pictures have no literary content, but consist of shapes or lines or dribbles or scratches or blots put down for their own sake and for whatever visual interest results. In the case of Jackson Pollock, for instance, the results have undeniable interest, but in a *plastic* sense. It is perfectly reasonable to claim that a series of lines is worth looking at and, like the poem, "does not *mean* but *be.*"

There also exists a group of painters called abstractionists who feel that, while a picture must grow organically and be important as an entity rather than as a substitute for the real thing (apple, tree, mountain, person), it must start from some place or thing in the objective world.

Some non-objectivists have been known to eschew training and study as a barrier to true expression. Some abstractionists are considerably inclined toward formal training.

In both schools there are sincere practitioners. There are also sincere and very gifted academicians, mystics, surrealists and supporters of the school of social consciousness, but we are discussing non-objectivists and abstractionists because they are pertinent to this moment. In each of these camps, as in all the others, there are also fakers and mountebanks and, most conspicuous of all, well-meaning and mediocre imitators. The genius, says Jacques Barzun, is hard to spot. "When alive he will probably defy recognition by signs. Either he resembles ordinary men too much for our storybook minds, or he gives so few proofs of worldly judgment that it is hard to credit him with any capacity whatever." We must take the mediocre with the genius and likely leave it to our grandchildren to recognize the latter. Things have usually worked that way.

It is eminently right that the present world of swiftly changing values, of unaccustomed juxtapositions, of general unpredictability should produce a subjective art — an art that comes from within. It is also inevitable that a flood of pallid imitators and even phonies should bring upon the school serious criticism. Finally, it is inevitable that the current pre-eminence of the non-objective in American art (it is the *avant garde*) should bring about revolt. It has.

Within the "silent" generation, in the art schools, is a large number of questioning students. They are not revolting against modern art, but against non-objective art which the less thoughtful call the "dribble and drool" school and the more thoughtful consider too accidental, lacking in direction, undisciplined, too negative for a society that, they are beginning to feel, needs a directive away from fear, hysteria and preoccupation with self-analysis. These young revolutionists are swinging away from the barely established *avant garde* toward a painting with what they choose to call more "content."

It is too early to say what face their own work will

assume. It will probably be abstract. It may even have over-tones of moralizing (which has never particularly benefited any art). However it develops, it will not be the product of a "silent" generation, but rather the product of a generation momentarily confused by its inheritance of appallingly confused issues.

1953

# Confession of Faith

Some years ago I gave a talk at one of the University convocations. It was not a religious gathering, and I had been asked to speak, for ten minutes, on ART. What actually happened was a peculiarly out-of-place confession of faith on my part.

Today we are participating in a service where that sort of thing *is* in order. I would like to continue my inconsistency, however, and devote a *part* of my time to art. When I have finished I hope you will be charitable and agree with me that in my own peculiar way I have spoken of matters appropriate to a chapel service.

First, let me make a statement: art, to an artist, is more than a technique of putting on paint. It is a way of life. And it can be purposeful and useful, or it can be circumscribed and worthless.

Second, let me give you a brief lecture on some recent art history.

During the last half of the Nineteenth Century the official and acceptable art of France — of Paris, which was the art capital of the world — had become so trite, so light-weight, so full of clichés, and so standardized in technique that it ceased altogether to be what living art must be — INVENTIVE.

There was a revolt by those artists beyond the official pale. The first and much maligned shock troops of the revolt were the French Impressionists — Seurat, Monet and the others. From the freedoms won by these men grew the concepts of the early giants of modern art — Cezanne, Gauguin, Van Gogh.

And from these have come the further explorations of the later greats — Picasso, Braque, Matisse.

Now, in all this recent history *one* thing is important above all others. The original Nineteenth Century revolt was in the field of *method,* new ways of painting, new techniques of applying color, new kinds of useful distortion. A revolt, in other words, having to do with *how* to paint and not *what* to paint. And since that time there has been a constant refinement, a reshuffling, a multitude of approaches, and almost always in one field of concentration — *how* to paint. The results, to some of you, are curious and alarming.

To an increasing number of present-day artists the results are alarming, too, and for probably different reasons.

These artists are awakening to the fact that over-long they have dwelt in ivory towers. They have indulged too long in repetitious imitations of their contemporary painter heroes. They are embarrassed to find themselves fostering as deadly and as constricting an academy as ever existed.

Again, as in the Nineteenth Century, and because of repetition, the forms of art (this time modern art) have become clichés — a fast standardizing phraseology which has only its own importance; is interesting only as a *way* of doing.

*How* to paint is no longer enough.

No one can successfully deny the importance of the explorations of those we have come to call the *modern* artists. They have greatly expanded our horizons and have presented us with new means of saying things. But *now* these revitalized tools must be put to use. It is time to SAY something.

I don't suppose many of you have realized that you are in the midst of another artistic revolution. After nearly half a century of intense interest in ways of painting, painters are emerging as social beings with opinions, even with suggestions.

There is an urgency in recent art, evidence that painters recognize the need of putting their abilities to use, in what appears to be a developing struggle between the idea of man as a free and happy agent and that of man as an individually insignificant number in an impersonal system.

Artists are assuming moral responsibilities. They are beginning to say, "This is right . . . this is wrong," instead of saying only, "These colors and shapes are, together, interesting and clever."

They are at last finding, possibly rediscovering, that they must serve, and help shape a PLAN for mankind bigger than themselves, a plan which involves choices between possible rights and possible wrongs, a plan that involves the greatest fruition of human hopes.

For a moment, now, let us keep this emerging situation in mind and turn to some other things.

These other things involve a sort of letting down of the hair. During my time here I have talked a great deal with a great many of you. Quite aside from the scandalous amount of coffee I have consumed in the process, it has been a highly rewarding experience. I have come to know you fairly well, a considerable reward in itself.

But there is one thing we don't touch upon as often as I could wish. Maybe I haven't had the wit to ask certain questions. I suspect most of you wouldn't have an answer. The question is, I'm afraid, rather pompous sounding. Anyway, this is it: To just what kind of star have you hitched your wagon?

I suppose, should I ask the question directly, you would say you hoped to be a doctor, or an engineer, or a teacher, or an educated tramp. That isn't what I mean. Those things aren't stars.

Maybe if you told me you plan to be a teacher and I asked you *why,* we'd get closer to it.

You are big boys and girls now. You are old enough to consider some of the stars. You are old enough to realize that a life dedicated to no truly big idea is in danger of going around in awfully small, awfully boring circles. It's not enough that you want to be teachers or engineers. There must be a purpose served thereby. Maybe if the purpose is big enough it won't matter too much which you are.

Why is it that some teachers, highly trained and technically competent, are such fizzles, such duds? Why are some mill hands so vital and important as people? I think it has something to do with this matter of getting involved with a star of the first magnitude.

There are all kinds of stars, of varying magnitudes.

Many people base their lives on some kind of fulfillment held out by the church. A few of them hope, quite literally, to make the grade into Heaven. A few mind their P's and Q's from day to day because of a gnawing and half-admitted fear that just possibly it might turn out that there *is* a Hell.

I have known people who, consciously or otherwise, have given their living over to the cause of one race or another — Negro, Gentile, Jew. Or to an economic group — the underdog, the common man, the aristocracy of wealth. Or have built their lives upon the furtherance of the concepts of a political group — Nazi, Communist, Socialist. Some live for the Second Coming of a Messiah, some for the First, some to disprove the validity of religion altogether.

Let me confess something. I'm not much worried about Heaven or Hell. I'm not entirely convinced that it isn't all a fancy man-made myth. I'm not dedicating my life to the interest of the underdog or the common man, and most certainly not to the maintenance of the aristocracy of wealth. I'm not a Nazi, or a Communist, or a Socialist — or a Republican. I'm not waiting for the First, or Second, or Third coming of a Messiah. I'm not out to push the Negroes, or the Gentiles, or the Jews, either up or down. Because what I believe excludes any difference among Negroes and Gentiles and Jews and Protestants and Catholics.

I believe in the Brotherhood of Man — *all* men. It's the biggest and shiniest and most breath-taking star in the firmament and the only one that has enough pull to save us from our tragically stupid and short-sighted selves.

And how does this concern art, or artists?

Well, some artists are aware of what it is and some aren't. Some are able to give it a name and some aren't, but what it is they are turning to now, at this moment in history, is faith in the eventual fulfillment of that brotherhood. Increasing numbers of them are painting, right now, about the desperate need to *remember* that man's brotherhood — and it has many other names — is what life is for.

Is it stupidly idealist to have faith in this thing? Are there any signs to bolster one's faith? My offerings of proof are only little ones. There are big ones on the other — some call it the devil's — side. But on my side, for example, are the artists. More and more they turn away from dry abstract considerations to paint that love and understanding are cleaner and stronger than war and hate, that man must understand *himself* and so set himself aright on the road to brotherhood.

Or the discussion group I heard about recently. A group of rabbis, Catholic priests, Protestant ministers and other men of all creeds and races asking direct and embarrassing questions of one another to find out what holds up the realization of brotherhood. Such questions as these: Why are you Jews that way about intermarriage? How come you Catholics supported Franco? Whoever told you Episcopalians you have a private pipe-line to Heaven? Or the sorority on this campus which chose to have its charter taken away rather than back down on its pledging of a black girl.

Yes, these are small things. I'm not kidding myself. There will be no brotherhood of man in my time, or my son's, or my son's son's. But when enough people recognize the star — when we Jews and we Gentiles and we Negroes and we Catholics discover that we are people, just that, then there won't be any more need for the threat of Hell or the promise of Heaven.

If you haven't found your star, consider this one.

1959